Architecture of the British Empire

Architecture of the British Empire

Jan Morris · Charles Allen · Gillian Tindall
Colin Amery · Gavin Stamp

Photographs by General Editor

Robert Fermor-Hesketh

The Vendome Press
New York

First published in the United States of America by
The Vendome Press, 515 Madison Avenue, New York, New York 10022

Distributed in the United States of America by
Rizzoli International Publications, Inc., 597 Fifth Avenue,
New York, New York 10017

Distributed in Canada by Methuen Publications

Library of Congress Cataloging in Publication Data

Architecture of the British Empire.
  Bibliography: P.
  Includes index.
  Contents: In Quest of the Imperial Style/Jan Morris—
A Home Away from Home/Charles Allen—Existential
Cities/Gillian Tindall—Public Buildings/Colin Amery—Church
Architecture/Gavin Stamp—Conclusion/Robert Fermor-Hesketh.
  1. Architecture, British. 2. Architecture, Modern—Great
Britain—Colonies. 1. Fermor-Hesketh, Robert.
NA964.A73   1986   720′.9171′241   86–5533
ISBN 0–86565–062–4

Designed by Helen Lewis

Typeset by Keyspools Ltd., Golborne, Lancs
Colour separations by Newsele Litho Ltd.
Printed in Italy by LEGO, Vicenza

Contents

For Jeanne, with love

Uitenhage church, South Africa, built in the mid-nineteenth century. It would originally have dominated its surroundings, but subsequent development has reduced its prominence.

Author's Acknowledgments

I WOULD PARTICULARLY LIKE TO THANK Dalu Jones for her invaluable advice
and tireless assistance in organizing the book, and Giles Eyre, Jan Pieper
and Robert Erskine, whose work contributed greatly to the final result.
Dr George Michell, Uma Dubash, Desmond Fitzgerald, Momin Latif, Cherry Leigh,
David and Lucy Grenfell, Claire and Alexander Hesketh, Tara Singh, Marjorie Crodelle,
Mark Miller-Mundy, Simon and Emma Keswick, Kenneth Diacre de Liancourt, David Towill
and Andrew Fraser all gave help or moral support at times when they were needed.
Geoff Wilkinson processed all the photographs, and Barry Taylor and Olympus
Cameras provided invariably efficient assistance with equipment.

All the maps, with the exception of the early map of Madras
on page 97, were kindly lent by the Royal Geographical Society.
For the Madras map I would like to thank the Bodleian Library, Oxford;
for the three architectural drawings on pages 149 and 152, the British Architectural
Library, R.I.B.A., London; for the photograph of Naini Tal Hill Station on page 190,
the National Army Museum; for the painting of Government House, Calcutta,
on page 128, and the photograph on page 62, Giles Eyre.
For the remainder of black and white photographs I am grateful to Charles Allen.

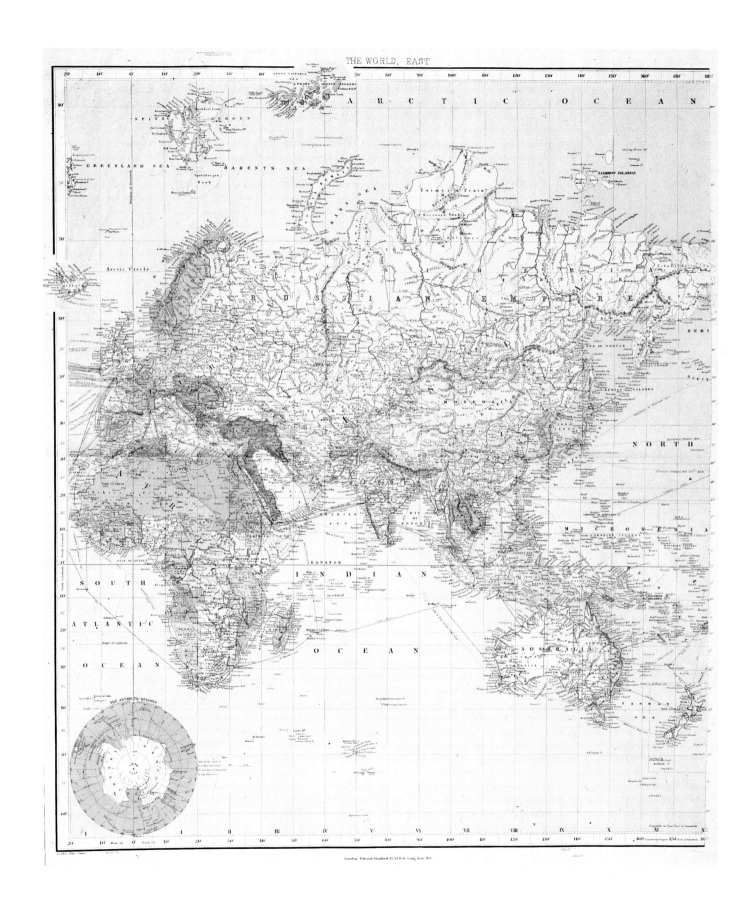

London: Edward Stanford, 12, 13 & 14, Long Acre, W.C.

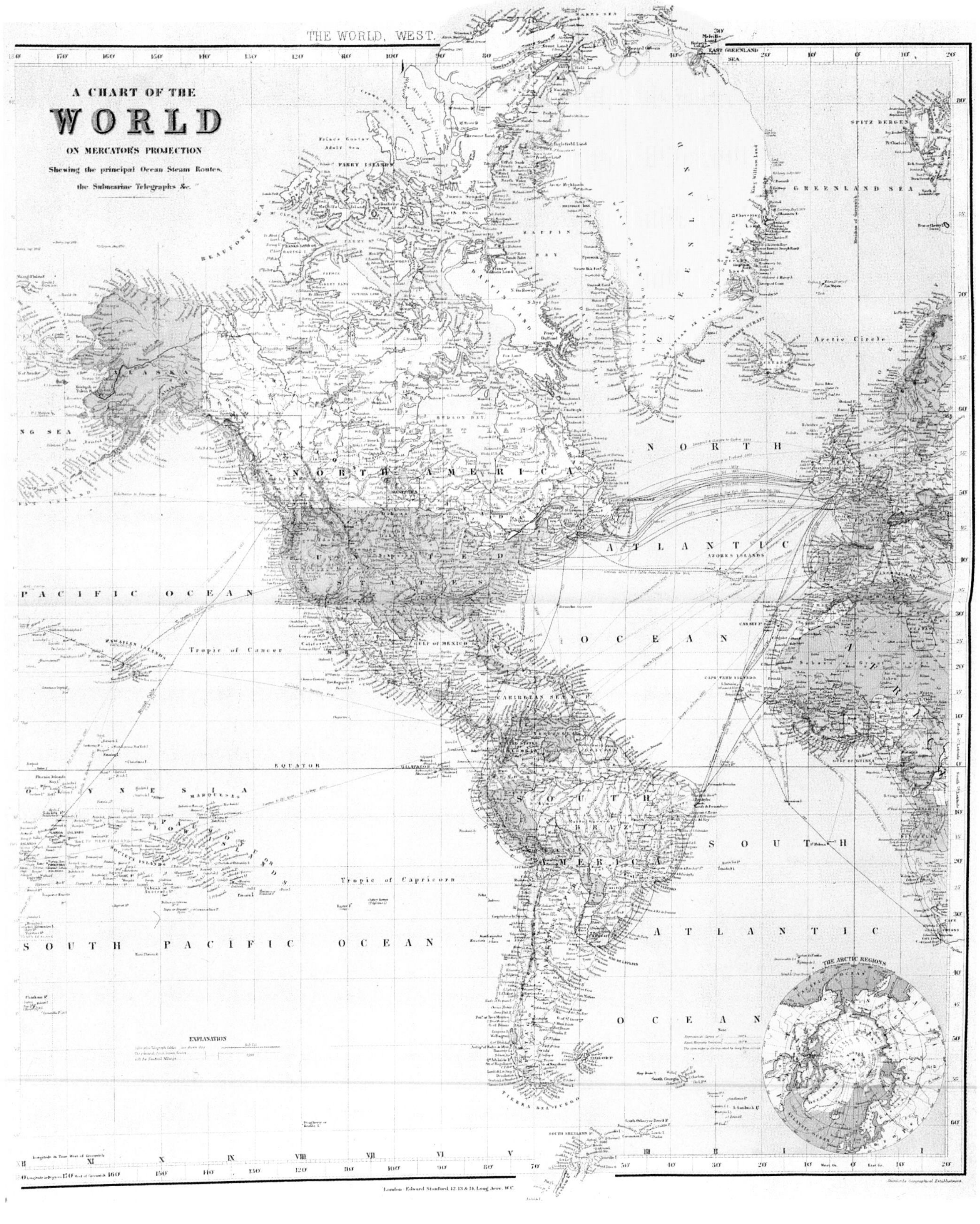

A CHART OF THE
WORLD
ON MERCATOR'S PROJECTION

Shewing the principal Ocean Steam Routes,

the Submarine Telegraphs &c.

NORTH AMERICA

UNITED STATES

SOUTH AMERICA

BRAZIL

GREENLAND

GREENLAND SEA

SPITZBERGEN

Arctic Circle

EAST GREENLAND SEA

BEAUFORT SEA

HUDSON BAY

BAFFIN BAY

NORTH ATLANTIC OCEAN

PACIFIC OCEAN

GULF OF MEXICO

CARIBBEAN SEA

AZORES ISLANDS

CANARY IS.

CAPE VERDE ISLANDS

GULF OF GUINEA

AFRICA

HAWAIIAN ISLANDS

Tropic of Cancer

EQUATOR

Tropic of Capricorn

POLYNESIA

MARQUESAS

NEW ZEALAND

SOUTH PACIFIC OCEAN

SOUTH ATLANTIC OCEAN

TIERRA DEL FUEGO

FALKLAND IS.

SOUTH SHETLAND

South Georgia

S. Sandwich I.

PARRY ISLAND

THE ARCTIC REGIONS

EXPLANATION

Submarine Telegraph Cables are shewn thus

The principal Ocean Steam Routes

with the Nautical Mileage

Longitude in Time West of Greenwich

XII   XI   X   IX   VIII   VII   VI   V

Longitude in Degrees West of Greenwich
180   170   160   150   140   130   120   90   80   70

West Gr.   0   East Gr.

London Edward Stanford, 12, 13 & 14, Long Acre, W.C.

Stanford's Geographical Establishment.

In Quest of the Imperial Style

Jan Morris

Park Street cemetery, Calcutta:
the alpha and omega of British imperial India.

EMPIRES COME, EMPIRES GO, and on the whole their intangibles last longest: manners, customs, ways of thought, beliefs. Altered and adapted by successor systems, developed into new techniques, perverted into superstition, degraded into parody, they are likely to survive when the last imperial palace is just a pile of stones, and the last imperial road is overlaid by motorway or grassed off the maps.

Architecture, nevertheless, is the badge of sovereignty, and when we look around our contemporary world we see its history visibly punctuated by the constructions of those particular peoples who have, over the centuries, imposed their styles and purposes upon the rest of mankind – memorials sometimes tremendous, sometimes merely wistful, of the imperial powers which one by one, as the Spaniard José Ortega y Gasset put it, went 'galloping down the highroad of history' leaving clouds of dust behind them. When the dust clears, the structures remain, if not for eternity, at least for a few centuries: and since they are less likely to be distorted than religions, systems of law or even languages, they remain the most accurate index of the imperial past, and can often tell us even more vividly than memoir or scholarly reconstruction what their builders were about.

Among the great empires of history the British was not the most imaginative in architecture, nor the boldest, but it was much the widest in scale and application. Short enough in duration – in effect, some 350 years from start to finish – it was unexampled in range. At its apogee, around the turn of the twentieth century, it ruled a quarter of the world's population and nearly a quarter of its land surface, not to mention, as the Colonial Office used to claim, 'nearly all the isolated islands and rocks in the ocean'. Previous empires had been much more narrowly contained by the techniques of their times, and by the state of human knowledge, and even the British Empire's contemporary rivals never matched the global interference of London in its heyday.

The British Empire embraced territories of every geographical kind, geological formation, climate, language, density of populace, state of development, sophistication of culture, warmth of local sympathy or chill of local distaste.

Sometimes the British were dealing with subject peoples of ancient civilization, sometimes with blank primitives. Sometimes they were there for commercial profit, sometimes for self-security, sometimes just to keep another empire out. In several of their possessions there arose substantial settlement colonies, with complete communities of expatriate Europeans, in others their authority was represented by a company or two of soldiers and a handful of bureaucrats in a peeling clapboard office. In the Canadian north-west their men in the field wore fur coats and swaggered about like Cossacks; in Africa they wore baggy shorts and were addressed as *bwana*; in India they spent much of their time wandering around in tented encampments; in the Caribbean they lived like medieval landowners surrounded by serfs. From the beginning to end, there was no pattern to the enterprise. Even its methods were muddled. Economically these fluctuated from the starkest protectionism to the grand ideals of Free Trade. Politically they groped intermittently towards some logical pattern of control or administration. Strategically it could well be argued that Britain would have been better off without an empire at all. The separate territories were governed in a hundred different ways, at one time or another, some of them moving gradually towards autonomy, some apparently destined to remain for ever absolute wards of London, and apologists for the imperial idea never did make it clear whether the Empire was primarily for the benefit of the British, or primarily for the improvement of the subject peoples, or just for the well-being of the world at large. It was, in Benjamin Disraeli's definition, 'the most peculiar of empires'.

Though it was at its climax unrivalled in its dominance, it was never omnipotent. It could never be said of the British that they had achieved mastery of the world, in the Roman sense. Other advanced civilizations, other Powers almost as Great, thrived alongside their own: in earlier years the Spaniards and the Dutch, in later years the French, the Russians, the Germans and the Americans, all posed powerful challenges to imperial supremacy. Though the British themselves were inclined to suppose, especially in the

*Lord Ripon, still in place in front of
the Ripon Building, Madras. Statues of his contemporaries
are now in the grounds of the zoo in Calcutta.*

opulence of their High Victorianism, that their tastes and values dominated the earth, it was not really so: even their early superiority in matters industrial and technical hardly lasted more than a generation or two. The climax of the British Empire was really a case of 'first among equals', and the decline which followed was certainly not the fall of another Rome, but merely the way the world was going.

All this was in the nature of British imperialism: terrific indeed in many ways, but essentially diffuse and pragmatic, even uncertain. It is no surprise then that the architecture of the Empire, too, was almost endlessly varied. Just as there was nothing definitive to the philosophy of this imperium, so there was nothing absolute to its building art. Many other cultures affected its manners of self-expression, and at one time or another its architecture embraced all European styles, from English Jacobean to International Modernist, besides every kind of local variant and adaptation.

There never was, consequently, a British Imperial Style to be listed in the architectural textbooks. All varied, as did the Empire itself, with time, with place, with circumstance. Spanning, as it did, not merely such immense physical limits but also three centuries of ever-accelerating change, the imperial architecture never had a chance to settle down. And in this too, we see now, it was truly an emblem of its sponsorship, for the Empire of the British never did find a satisfactorily organic role for itself, and in the end was dissolved not by hostile force or moral self-denial, but chiefly by lack of conviction.

Corner shop, Cape Town, late nineteenth century: a very rare surviving example of the elaborately decorated buildings common on corner sites in South Africa and Australia.

*Private house, Black River, Jamaica. Black River, built at the turn
of the century, was once a prosperous community, but it was
constructed of wood and has not survived well.*

14

Clarendon, near Launceston, Tasmania,
built by James Cox in the late 1830s.

The buildings of an empire are not, by and large, quite like other buildings. Their intentions are different, and their poses too, for one is unlikely to be altogether natural, or totally oneself, when settling in another country – still less when seizing it! British imperial architecture was an architecture of exiles, and was seldom absolutely identical with contemporary design at home. A country mansion was never quite the same if slave labour built it; a church acquired a different spirituality if it stood in a heathen wasteland; it was no good transplanting an English sub-urban villa to the Punjab, not just because of the weather, but also because, in India, at least a dozen servants would be thought necessary to run it. Most importantly of all, it was the fact of imperialism itself, the uninvited presence of aliens on a foreign shore, which gave to the buildings of the overseas Empire a vaguely discernible unity.

Through their houses or places of pleasure, for instance, we may see how those self-conscious adventurers regarded their status among the indigenes. Sometimes, having escaped perhaps from more modest circumstances at home, they saw themselves as an aristocracy, and built themselves homes which proclaimed them to be, among the foliage of some wilder parkland, colonial equivalents of dukes and earls at home. Or they were anxious to convince themselves of their cultural superiority, and so consciously used Doric columns or Composite entablatures to announce their

Lady Pepperrell House, near Kittery, Maine,
built by Lady Mary Pepperrell in 1760.

pedigree or refinement. Or they wanted to accentuate their racial separateness, always an instrument of British imperialism, surrounding their houses with high walls or wide compounds to keep the locals at arm's length, and arranging pleasure retreats on high and inaccessible ridges.

Their buildings of authority, too, displayed often enough the particular characteristics of this dominion. They were generally more serviceable than spectacular, this being an empire that prided itself on practical economy. Few British military engineers combined mechanical skills with ornamental artistry, like the great Italian and French fortifiers; the residences of imperial Governors were country houses more often than palaces. Taste as well as economy decreed that administrative buildings were generally unostentatious, though there were exceptions: the New Zealand Government building at Wellington was claimed to be the biggest wooden structure in the world, while Sir Edwin Lutyens observed of the offices at Simla, summer capital of British India, that if they had been built by monkeys, 'one would have said, "what clever monkeys, they must be shot in case they do it again" '.

Rather more ebullient, since the fundamental purpose of this empire was material profit, was the architecture of industry and expansion – the docks, the warehouses, the bridges, above all the railways which advertised British enterprise and inventiveness across the world, and kept the imperial revenues on the move. These were the works that seemed to cry, as the Welsh-Australian Prime Minister William Morris Hughes cried in 1918, 'What other worlds have we to conquer? We are like so many Alexanders!' The teeming ports of the British, greeting the world's shipping in every continent – the towering granaries of Canada or jute mills of Bombay; mighty irrigation works in Africa and India; railroads which ran wherever a locomotive would go, up mountains, through jungles, to end in railway stations of flamboyant display – these were contructions of a grandeur to match the achievements of the ancients, and gave British imperialists too, now and then, Ozymandian illusions of eternity.

Neither command, though, nor plain profit satisfied the imperial instinct in the later years of the adventure, when the British people succeeded in convincing themselves that the Empire was actually an instrument of God's purpose. As evangelical religion transformed the face and temper of England itself, so it gave a new meaning to the architecture of empire. The British Empire was never a missionary agency, proudly stressing indeed its official tolerance of all faiths, but in a general way it sought to proselytize by example, and its improving aims were plainly written in its buildings.

The imperial churches naturally proclaimed the Providential nature of this empire, whether they were perched above bluffs on tough Atlantic shores, white and pristine beside oriental parks, blistered in the African bush or unabashedly steepled, like the church of St George down river from the Taj Mahal, among the supreme masterpieces of non-Christian design. Hardly less inspirational of intent, though, were many other kinds of imperial building; indeed as the Victorian century passed *most* imperial structures came to convey some didactic impulse or other. A court of law suggested not merely justice but salvation too: consider the example on the foreshore at Madras, which was actually surmounted by a lighthouse, like a beacon of redemption! Market halls habitually incorporated exhortatory emblems of diligence, like scythes or fishing nets, and government buildings were decorated with images of Fair Trade or Racial Harmony; and when they built a new Parliament at Ottawa, in Canada, in 1866, it was modelled partly upon a Gothic chapter house and partly on the Oxford Museum.

And in the end these somewhat obvious messages were to be most powerfully conveyed not by individual buildings at all but by the stance of whole imperial cities. The British might not be the greatest imperial builders of history, but they were unquestionably the greatest builders of imperial cities. In time their empire became overwhelmingly an urban empire. Its centres of power and profit generally clustered around the seaports, at the mouths of great rivers, and so there arose along the coasts of the world a series of remarkable British conurbations, many of them started absolutely from scratch: Philadelphia, Baltimore, Van-

*The Government Offices, Simla, to which
Sir Edwin Lutyens took great exception.*

*The timber-framed Post Office, Simla,
described as 'Wild West Gothic' in style.*

couver, Sydney, Melbourne, Auckland, Hong Kong, Singapore, Karachi, Calcutta, Bombay – all of these and many more were the creations of British imperialism, built where nothing existed before but a few simple fishing huts, or a huddle of ferrymen's shacks.

Such cities still provide the best imperial indices of all, and express better than anything the paradoxical mixture of opportunism and piety which became the final hallmark of British sovereignty. Allegories not always apparent on a territorial scale were easier to perceive at a civic level, and by Victorian days the municipal pride of the Empire was almost as grand, and just as educational, as the pride of empire as a whole. Stamford Raffles, the founder of Singapore, wanted to write the name of Britain 'in characters of light', to endure when 'her triumphs shall have become an empty name'. Half a century later the city fathers of Bombay liked to boast that their municipal record of health and hygiene was better than London's. The logical planning which was characteristic of the imperial cities everywhere was an exhibition of the way life itself might be if the imperial tenets were properly honoured and the best imperial chances grasped.

In the elementary years of British imperialism its architecture was purely eclectic. How the imperialists built depended entirely upon where they were, and why, and they certainly did not erect their houses, offices and forts to illustrate any central conception of imperialism.

Often enough in the early years of settlement they were perfectly prepared to live as the natives did – indeed they never gave up the Bengali bungalow, building derivations of it everywhere from Hong Kong to Jamaica. More often, however, when they had passed through the first hut-on-the-beach or log-cabin stage, they made themselves structures more or less of the kinds they knew at home. The simplest were in plain English rural style, recognizably medieval in origin, but the more elaborate did have architectural pretensions; and since those were the days of

Classical Revival, derivations of Greek and Roman designs, in varying degrees of scholasticism, proliferated wherever the British settled.

In the colonies of the American seaboard the settlers developed the elegant form later to be know as American Colonial – ironically perhaps, for it was to become almost a declaration of republican independence. Based sometimes on country house architecture in England, sometimes more simply upon rustic vernaculars, it was implanted also in Bermuda, the Caribbean and even, in cruder forms, in steamy settlements of Guiana and Honduras. There was nothing very original to it actually, but translated into foreign settings, built of unfamiliar materials and established in such novel circumstances, it was to blossom into a genre all its own.

Mount Pleasant, Philadelphia. A private house built in 1761–2 by John Macpherson, a Scottish privateer, Mount Pleasant was described by John Adams as 'the most elegant country seat in Pennslyvania' when he visited it in 1775.

The Dock Street Theatre, Charleston, South Carolina, a restoration
of the original 1736 building on the site.

Lemon Hill, Fairmount Park, Philadelphia, commissioned by
Henry Platt in the mid-eighteenth century.

*Country residence of the British Governor-General
at Barrackpore, West Bengal.*

In Australia, in the years of convict settlement, the British devised other variations of nostalgic classicism, notably in Tasmania, where fine stone mansions were built by convict workmen to the designs of convict architects – country houses of curiously solidified English allusion, attended by their own English-style inns and parish churches, and encircled by oaks, elms, beeches, poplars and hawthorns especially brought from home. In India the nabobs built themselves immensely grand Palladian town houses and suburban villas, profuse in not always accurate detail, with mock-marble columns and lordly fenestration – buildings proper to dynasties of imperial merchant princes, and surprisingly well suited, as it happened, to the heat and blinding sunshine of Bengal.

Elsewhere English taste was subtly mutated by local circumstance. In South Africa it was tempered sometimes by Afrikaner idioms, in Mauritius and the Caribbean French preferences showed, and in the ports of the Indian south one sometimes found gabled or wide-eaved reminders of Holland. Still, they were mostly recognizably English buildings that the seventeenth- and eighteenth-century Empire built, and in fact the imperial architecture depended heavily upon manuals of design sent out from London.

Churches in particular, all over the Empire, were derived from the plans of James Gibbs, designer of St Martin-in-the-Fields in London, and if there was one single building plan which might be said to epitomize the pre-Victorian Empire almost everywhere, it was Gibbs' gracefully simple pattern for a Christian church. A neat Georgian job, steepled and porticoed, it was to appear in various applications, for the uses of differing sects, in a staggering variety of environments – Nova Scotia to South Africa, India to New South Wales – the most widely distributed prototype, it is probably safe to say, in the entire history of religious architecture.

*An eighteenth-century shop house,
Lucea, Jamaica.*

Later, as the Victorian century unfolded into its grand amplitude, and Classical gave away to Gothic among progressive architects at home, the search for a more explicitly imperial style set in. By then the difficult American colonies had been lost, and the Empire was altogether more imperial. The remaining white settlements were staunchly loyal to the crown, except for their enclaves of refractory foreigners, and were gradually to move towards self-government within the imperial fold. The subject colonies, ranging in size, importance and interest from the subcontinent of India to almost imperceptible coaling-stations, were all firmly under control. Theorists began to conceive for the Empire a permanent, rational shape, and to see it as one invulnerable and self-sustaining superpower.

The idea of an architectural style to match these aspirations certainly entered their thoughts – indeed in 1834 the architect J. M. Gandy drew up plans for a central Imperial Palace of marvellous symbolism – and when, after the Battle of the Styles at home, Gothic became the generally established High Victorian idiom, it was eagerly adopted as an imperial medium too. Like an invading army itself, it swept across the British possessions, rearing its pinnacles, turrets and finials wherever the flag flew.

In many ways it was very suitable for the purpose. Conceived though it was in wet and windy northern Europe, it proved surprisingly amenable to emigration. It looked properly defiant among the snows of Canada. It looked proudly aldermanic in the Australian sun. With its plethora of detail it was oddly at ease with the indigenous architectures of the east. It really did have an imperial look, dominant, assured, besides convincingly representing, with its Ruskinian inferences of divine favour, the evangelical side of the imperial mission. So far as the white settlement colonies were concerned, it was the nearest they ever got to an imperial style, for thereafter they built their buildings like any other independent peoples, following international fashions of design, and sometimes producing developments of their own.

It was not, though, the last stylistic word for the British Empire as a whole. Sir Osbert Sitwell once fancied in the half-oriental look of the Brighton Pavilion a 'dormant' British Empire style: in fact by the middle of the nineteenth century the imperial architects had been feeling their way towards some such synthesis, if rather less fantastic, of east and west, rulers and ruled. The old hubris of Empire was somewhat tempered by then, and the imperialists pined for forms which would imply a blend of command and cooperation. So it came about that the most truly archetypal buildings of the British Empire, such as they were, went up in the dependent territories of the east.

Aesthetically they were always difficult to categorize, for they were essentially hybrids. Upon a European foundation, sometimes Gothic, sometimes Classical, oriental forms were grafted, in the best examples, with an organic thoroughness, in weaker works just by decorative veneer. They were called in their time Indo-Saracenic, Hindu Gothic, Renaissance Mogul, and in one sort or another, from late Victorian days until the dispersal of British power after the Second World War, they were strewn all across the eastern empire from Dar-es-Salaam (where Government House was a mock-Moorish palace) to Kuala Lumpur (where the Secretariat was a handsome mongrel of Islamic and Italianate breeding, with a railway station like a mosque up the road, and a club in purest half-timbered Tudor bang opposite).

The culmination of this movement, as of the imperial constructions as a whole, was the palace of the Viceroys built by Edwin Lutyens for the new Indian capital of New Delhi. Begun in 1914, this was fine, but too late. A conciliatory marriage of Classical and Mogul forms, with a touch of the Buddhist too, it was one of the greatest palaces ever built – larger than Versailles, and the one truly colossal official building erected by the British during their generations of overseas suzerainty. Yet even as it rose, the British Empire progressed towards its inevitable end. Before it was finished the chief agent of the Empire's fall, Mahatma Gandhi, was being entertained as an equal within its walls: within twenty years of its completion the British had withdrawn from India altogether, and the vast ramshackle mechanism of their empire, which never did achieve that rational unity they dreamed for it, had fallen apart for ever.

*Railway station and administrative buildings, Kuala Lumpur,
once described as 'Anglo-marzipan' in style.*

Town villa, Kuala Lumpur, late nineteenth century.

*Allidina Visram High School, Mombasa, founded in 1918
with money provided by the Aga Khan Community.
The architect and masons were brought over from India.*

'*Look on these works, ye Mighty, and despair!*' There is irony always to the images of empire, when the glory is lost, the idea is discredited, and powers that thought themselves eternal have proved mortal after all. Even in 1940 Winston Churchill could imagine the British Empire lasting another thousand years: yet it is gone already, and so are many of its buildings, some vanished altogether, some to be found half-crumbled into tenements, obliterated by tower blocks, or converted into humbler uses (like the great Madras Club, once a very temple of imperial consequence, eventually used for the storage of newsprint). They were not always built of very resilient materials; they were often in places of corrosive climate; and they were, after all, only particles in that transient cloud of dust.

Enough remains, nevertheless, to offer us a revealing if tantalizing register, as in the pages of this book, of the rise and fall of an empire – and that the biggest empire of all, and perhaps of its explicit kind the last. Great cities like Melbourne or Bombay still preserve for us the virtues, the weaknesses, the absurdities and the splendours of the imperial career. Lovely white houses of Virginia or New England remind us of its old contradictions. Bungalows of the Indian plains tell us how the imperialists sweated homesick in the field. Railway stations, bridges, tunnels, canals, speak to us as majestically of this empire's nature as do the great Roman roads of another dominion long before. It is less than 370 years, after all, since the first successful British overseas colony was established upon the Virginian shore: many stones of empire still remain to move the passer-by and enlighten the historian.

The British Empire did not produce many great architects or planners of its own, and only a handful of well-

Y.M.C.A., Chowringhee Road, Calcutta.

Standard Bank, Pietermaritzburg, designed by the Natal architect
P. M. Dudgeon in 1889. Although conceived on a small scale,
the building gives an impression of considerable stature.

known names are recalled by its constructions: a few expatriates, like William Light in Adelaide, Francis Greenway in Sydney, John Coleman in Singapore, John Garstin, F. W. Stevens and William Emerson in India, and a few visiting eminences, like Walter Burley Griffin in Australia, Lutyens and Herbert Baker in India and Africa, or the ubiquitous Gilbert Scotts. Nor did it create many masterpieces: the architectural handbooks, if they do not record a British Imperial Style, do not draw our attention to many British imperial examples, either. But it was an empire of terrific corporate personality, especially perhaps in the fulfilment of its Victorian self-esteem, and this strength of character still fitfully infuses the imperial relics.

Their various forms may not add up to one style, yet there is often something unmistakable to them all the same. Robert Byron, surveying the Empire's climactic architecture, once called it 'a permanent nineteenth century', but it is more specific than that: it is a masonry-and-ironwork Britishness, a material evocation of all the values, good or bad, enviable or insufferable, which made those off-shore islanders from northern Europe, for a few startling generations, so anomalously pre-eminent.

31

A Home Away from Home

Charles Allen

'EMIGRATION MAY BE REGARDED as a severe duty performed at the expense of personal enjoyment.' So declares the authoress of *Roughing it in the Bush* and *Life in the Clearings*, reiterating in that phrase 'severe duty' one of the characteristic leitmotifs of the British colonial experience. She was Mrs Susanna Moodie, who left England with her husband in 1832 to settle in Upper Canada. 'In most instances', Mrs Moodie continues, 'emigration is a matter of necessity, not of choice. Few educated persons accustomed to the refinement and luxuries of European Society ever willingly relinquish these advantages.'

But Mrs Moodie was wrong. As the nineteenth century wore on it was remarkable how many rather than how few 'educated persons accustomed to the refinement and luxuries of European Society' actually took the colonial plunge. The phenomenon of British colonial expansion and settlement, so often portrayed as a proletarian experience, is essentially the history of the British middle classes on the move. Mrs Moodie's husband was himself an army officer on half pay, part of that ever-growing and overstocked pool made up in large part of second sons of the manse from Scotland and Protestant Ireland, as well as the younger sons of English country gentry. It was this well educated, often ambitious work force, with high expectations but also conscious of the fact that prospects for advancement in Britain were limited, that supplied the colonies with their civil and military officers, as well as the first waves of their pioneer settlers, a phenomenon nicely summed up by the historian James Mill's remark that India provided 'a vast

system of outdoor relief for Britain's upper classes'.

The young gentlemen who made up this middle-class work force shared a common goal: to secure for themselves respectable, financially rewarding livings which would allow them to maintain those 'luxuries of European Society' to which they had been accustomed. Their main concern, in essence, was to continue a middle-class style of living overseas, not necessarily following middle-class occupations but seeking middle-class domesticity in middle-class homes. Where they differed was in the means to secure this goal. One category became temporary colonials, and spent their working lives as a privileged minority of civil or military officers in one or other of the many British colonies or protectorates lying between the Tropics of Cancer and Capricorn. The other category were bona fide colonists in the classical sense, settlers intent on establishing themselves in permanent holdings – usually but not exclusively in the more temperate, more English-like zones – that were intended to be all but independent of the mother country.

What both groups brought to the colonies, tropical or temperate, was an essentially middle-class belief in the virtues of 'severe duty', tempered with an equally characteristic desire for 'refinement and luxuries'. The architecture and domestic arrangements of the British overseas reflect these two key elements in various proportions, with 'severe duty' maintaining the upper hand in the early stages but gradually giving way to softer living. From these seemingly contradictory impulses emerged what might be called a 'colonial style' of architecture, modified to a greater or lesser degree by the use of local building materials and local or native architectural traditions.

'Severe duty' and 'refinement and luxuries' in their more extreme forms are present in the domestic architecture of the first British Empire, which was brought to an abrupt end with the surrender of Lord Cornwallis and his troops at Yorktown, Virginia, in October 1781. The foundations of this early empire were laid by Protestant settlers in Ireland in the sixteenth and seventeenth centuries, where they established their 'plantations' in the face of strong native opposition, to become a dominant majority in the north and a land-owning minority in the south. The experiment was repeated in the American colonies, with the Puritans dominating New England and a slave-owning plantocracy controlling the southern colonies of Virginia, Maryland, Carolina and, ultimately, Georgia. Nowhere was 'severe duty' better represented than in New England, and nowhere were 'refinement and luxury' more in evidence than in the 'great houses' of the southern colonies.

The Puritans had come to America to make a clean break with the past, but while they prided themselves on their independent and non-conformist spirit they were bound to look back over their shoulders, across the Atlantic. So it was that they named their farming communities after English towns and modelled them on the English village, centred on the village green and the place of worship, here renamed 'meeting house' in keeping with the Puritan creed. Nor were the homes they built for themselves mere shacks or even the log-cabins so closely identified with frontier occupation in America, which only became popular in the eighteenth century after being introduced by Scandinavian settlers along the Delaware River. The houses they put up were built to last and they echoed the heavy medieval forms of the cottages of the East Anglian countryside that they had left behind: narrow 'two up and two down' structures built around a central chimney, with thick oak frames, steeply pitched roofs and gable ends. Moreover, they were built to professional standards, using pit-sawn wood with mortice-

The House of the Seven Gables, probably built in about 1635.
Despite its apparent suitability, there is considerable doubt
as to whether Nathaniel Hawthorne used the house as a model
for his novel of the same name.

and-tenoned beams, often with imported bricks. Only when thatch and half-timbered walls proved unequal to the extremes of the New England climate were they replaced

Bacon's Castle, Surrey County, Virginia, built by Arthur Allen c1655, but later named after Nathaniel Bacon, who was to make his name in the 1676 Rebellion. It could have been built anywhere in England in the first four decades of the seventeenth century.

with what has quite rightly come to be regarded as characteristically American: unpainted clapboard walls topped by shingles and tiles, creating an effect that was plain and unpretentious and thoroughly in keeping with the New England spirit.

As the heroic age of the Puritan settlement of New England, the era of 'severe duty', gives way to easier times, so the austere look of their homes and public buildings softens in appearance into more open and more hospitable dwellings. We see sash windows replacing narrow casements, roofs becoming less steeply pitched, and the houses themselves growing wider. In Massachusetts this development often took the form of the 'salt-box' cottage in which the roof at the back was extended to cover additional rooms for larger families and more possessions. Poor overland communications between one settled area and another made it inevitable that a variety of building styles would develop, each typifying the characteristics, origins and occupations of its own community. By contrast, in the towns the tightening of the colonial hold by the British authorities encouraged greater standardization, helped by the sale of do-it-yourself pattern books designed specifically for the colonial market.

As Puritan decorum is replaced in the eighteenth century by Georgian display, so both town and country houses in the American colonies grow noticeably more spacious and formal in appearance. Wood gives way to brick and bricks to stone or stucco; central hearths are pushed to the side to make way for imposing hallways and grand staircases; front doors are reinforced with pilasters and classical porticos. The end result is the emergence of a distinctive American Colonial style, still modest by metropolitan standards but clearly designed to impress and signal success, typified by high basements below, roof balustrades above and, in between, a façade of stucco brick to give the appearance of smooth stone. Such a mansion was best sited on some prominent elevation in a landscaped country park: the residence of a landed colonial gentleman, perhaps, or the 'great house' of a southern planter, dominating a tamed landscape as its owner dominated his slave labour force.

Stratford, Montross, Virginia. The house was built
between 1725 and 1730 for Thomas Lee, and
was the birthplace of Robert E. Lee.

ABOVE *A late eighteenth-century house,*
Charleston, South Carolina.

OPPOSITE *Casa Loma, Toronto. North America's largest*
castle was built by the industrialist
Sir Henry Pellatt in 1911–14.

The phenomenon of the 'great house' was by no means confined to the North American colonies. Nowhere was it more starkly at odds with the surrounding countryside than in those other slave-based plantations of the Americas in the West Indies, where sugar was king and the sugar barons answerable to few regulations other than their own. Some of the wealthiest members of this plantocracy were from long-established English landowning families. Their ties with England were strong, and in consequence they looked to Britain for their architects and their building materials, although local woods were often incorporated to great effect. A case in point is Rose Hall in Jamaica, built in 1780 by a planter for his new bride, with 'floors and stairs, wainscoting and ceilings, doors and windows of mahogany, cedar, rosewood, ebony, orange and other native hardwoods of various colours, highly polished and well ar-ranged'. Many of these 'great houses' were extremely imposing in appearance. At Rose Hall 'spacious piazzas and corridors ran round the house above and below, the front door [being] reached by a very elegant double flight of stone steps'.

The Jamaican countryside to the east of Rose Hall is littered with the shells of other 'great houses' that went by such grandiloquent names as Good Hope, Bryan Castle, Mahogany Hall, Windsor Castle and Vale Royal, each the central hub of an estate made up of a sugar mill and a number of attendant slave villages. The central drawing room at Good Hope once sported an Adam frieze and elegant Palladian-style windows that no doubt helped to circulate the humid air. Outside in the garden a fine stone-cut counting house, built in the purest Georgian style, also served as a punishment cell for recalcitrant slaves.

Rose Hall, Jamaica, built by John Palmer in 1780. Despite the outward confidence and wealth of his creation, Palmer took the precaution of providing the basement rooms with loopholes for defence.

*Devon House, Kingston, Jamaica. A black Jamaican, George Steibel, who
made his fortune in South America, built the house
in 1881 and may also have designed it.*

OVERLEAF *'Gingerbread house', Black River, Jamaica.*

*Methodist manse, Falmouth, Jamaica, built in 1799 by
the Barretts, grandparents of Elizabeth Barrett Browning. The elegant
wrought-iron balconies were imported from Philadelphia.*

With 'rum and sugar enough belonging to him to make all the water in the Thames into punch', the West Indian sugar-planter is one of the stock figures of the first British Empire at its zenith – together with that of the Calcutta nabob and the North American landowner as personified by General George Washington, with his 3,200-acre Mount Vernon estate and his 115 black slaves. All three types represent the limits of that sought-after colonial goal of 'refinement and luxuries' taken to its furthest extreme – and in each case they also mark the end of an era. In North America the American colonies won their independence; in India the East India company was transformed from a trading to a governing body; and in the West Indies the sugar industry went into a slow decline as the result of increased competition from the French, increased taxation and the loss of trade with America after 1782. Sugar had ceased to be king long before that summer night in 1834 when 'freedom at midnight' finally ended slavery in the British West Indies. By then a combination of tropical hurricanes, sudden squalls, constant humidity and white ants had already seen to it that few of the 'great houses' of the previous century would survive into the next.

41

Deloraine, Nakuru: a fine early
twentieth-century example of settlers' architecture
in the White Highlands of Kenya.

The great house made its final appearance on the imperial scene in Africa, for it was Kenya that was ultimately to provide 'outdoor relief for Britain's upper classes' in full measure. It is recorded that in the first year of its opening in 1905 the Norfolk Hotel, in the newly laid out railhead out-station of Nairobi, accommodated no less than one marquis, three earls, five lords and three counts besides innumerable sporting gentlemen. To re-create the role of pathfinder that the morally doubtful Captain MacArthur had played in New South Wales exactly a century earlier there was the equally dubious figure of Hugh Cholmondeley, third Baron Delamere, who after a wild and misspent youth first entered Kenya on camel-back in 1897 and four years later secured a ninety-nine-year grant on a parcel of land in the uninhabited high country west of the Aberdere

Range. In what soon became known as the White Highlands or, more popularly, Happy Valley on account of the relaxed attitudes and morals of its leading personalities, Delamere was joined by other adventurers in the rapid settlement of this isolated country, made possible by the building of the extraordinary 'lunatic express' railway line from the coast to Lake Victoria.

In the Subukia Valley, for instance, a secluded and hitherto uninhabited – except by wandering Masai – cul-de-sac in the Kenya Highlands, the first land was taken up by white settlers in 1909. By 1928 there were thirty-eight European landowners growing maize and coffee and herding cattle, and a country club with thirty-two members. One such settler was Sir Michael Blundell, who when he first came to Subukia in 1925 lived in a *banda* of the most

42

primitive type. A quarter of a century later he was living in a comfortable stone-walled and tiled farmhouse, set in a landscaped English country garden which would not have disgraced a successful Surrey stockbroker. According to the Subukia Farmers' Association, a man 'of the right type' ought to be able to make good on a capital of £1000.

The exotic lifestyles of these white farmers were witnessed with mute but observant astonishment by the writer Evelyn Waugh in the 1920s. When he came to write his *Sword of Honour* trilogy he chose to give its amiable hero, the aristocratic Guy Crouchback, the background of a failed Kenya farmer. Meeting his former wife in later years, Guy recalls the 'old times' they once shared:

The group of bungalows that constituted their home, timber-built, round stone chimneys and open English hearth, furnished with wedding presents and good old pieces of furniture from the lumber rooms at Broome; the estate, so huge by European standards, so modest in East Africa, the ruddy earth roads, the Ford van and the horses; the white-gowned servants and their naked children always tumbling in the dust and sunshine round the kitchen quarters . . . Evening baths in the lake, dinner parties in pyjamas with their neighbours. Race Week in Nairobi, all the flagrant, forgotten scandals of the Muthaiga club, fights, adulteries, arson, bankruptcies, card-sharping, insanity, suicides, even duels – the whole Restoration scene re-enacted by farmers, eight thousand feet above the steaming seaboard.

*Cottage, Muthaiga, Nairobi. Built by Henderson, 'the' local architect,
it is very much in the English country cottage style
favoured by settlers in the Twenties.*

It was Kenya's leading gin palace, the rambling, pink-walled Muthaiga Club, which confined its membership exclusively to the landowning class, that provided the main rallying point and safety valve for this highborn, hard-living community. Many of its weaker members were wiped out by the collapse of raw commodity markets and prices in the wake of the 1930 slump – as were many rubber planters in Malaya and tea planters in Assam – but those who hung on were later to enjoy two comfortable decades of prosperity before Kikuyu discontent over 'stolen' land exploded into open revolt in the Mau Mau uprising of 1952, signalling the approaching end of British colonial rule in Africa and the dissolution, already begun in India in 1947, of the second British Empire.

In the African context it is worth noting that British penetration up-country into the bush produced no amalgam of styles, local and imported, as occurred in India and south-east Asia. This was due in large part to the fact that this 'pacification', to use the popular Victorian euphemism for occupation, of the African hinterland only really got under way in the last decades of the nineteenth century. The up-country traders in their 'barter-rooms' and 'canteens' in West Africa and the administrators who followed, not only in West Africa but also in East and Central Africa, all set up house in the local native thatch dwellings known in Swahili-speaking areas as *banda*, rudimentary mud-and-thatch beehive huts.

When the time came for these first-stage dwellings to be replaced, standardization had already laid its dead hand on government architecture in the form of the Public Works Department, whose officers were discouraged from employing initiative or applying vernacular embellishments, and were constantly required to tailor their plans to meet local government budgets. Cost-effectiveness was everything, and never more so than in Africa where such budgets were almost entirely dependent on local revenue based on minimal taxation. When the educationalist Mrs Sylvia Leith-Ross first accompanied her husband to Zungeru, the newly established capital of Northern Nigeria, in 1907 they were accommodated in standard government bungalows that had been shipped in sections from England and then erected by the PWD with local labour. 'They were all of one type', she writes in a private memoir. 'One could find them everywhere with exactly the same lack of amenities. They consisted of three rooms and a wide verandah all round. I had realised exactly what the bungalows would be like so it seemed perfectly natural to me, but they were even uglier than I thought they would be and devoid of any furniture except some large and heavy tables and a *punkah*, which was, so to speak, a petticoat attached to a long parallel pole which was swung back and forth by a small boy sitting on the verandah.' Both verandah and *punkah* exemplify the dominant role of India as the leading source of architectural models in colonial up-country architecture.

All civil and military officers travelling out to Africa at this period were required to take with them everything that they would require for the duration of their tour of service, much of it consisting of *chop* boxes containing food. In 1907 Captain Leith-Ross was thus entitled to 'eighty carriers for his tour of eighteen months, which meant eighty loads of fifty-six pounds, because fifty-six pounds was supposed to be the normal weight that a native carrier could carry with ease'. Much of their furniture was in the form of camping equipment – 'a camp chair, a camp stool, a camp bed with a cork mattress and a tin bath with a cover and a wickerwork lining into which you packed all your toilet necessities' – since the practice of touring the district – known variously as *ulendo*, 'going on trek' or 'going to bush' – was considered to be one of the most vital ingredients of good government in the colonies. In Sarawak and in other watery corners of the Empire touring was principally by way of the rivers, with officials sleeping in local village longhouses; in Africa much of it was done on foot, with the nights spent either under canvas or, in West Africa, in thatch *banda* rest-houses. In India, however, touring was conducted on a far grander scale, in keeping with the Mogul tradition from which the custom was descended. 'Going on tour' invariably took place during the 'cold weather' months. Part of it was spent under canvas in elaborate camps that included tented offices, dining quarters, sleeping quarters, bathrooms and

Barnum House, Grafton, Ontario, built in
1817 by Colonel Eliakim Barnum,
a loyalist who emigrated from Vermont.

latrines and always with a full complement of servants in the Indian manner; part of it moving along a circuit of bungalows, *pukka* and *kutcha*, that every major service had built for itself within its district.

What did survive from this first British Empire to become a lynchpin of the second was the institution of the up-country civil and military station or, to put it more plainly, the district headquarters. This simple but formidably practical institution was to find its apotheosis in nineteenth-century British India, but an early example can be found in Jamaica in the little country town of Mandeville. It sports a village green, a quaint stone church and a neat eighteenth-century court house said to be an exact replica of the custom house that stands on the wharf at Poole harbour in Dorset.

With the loss of its American colonies, Britain's colonizing energies were redirected elsewhere - principally, but not exclusively, towards the East. Upper Canada, later renamed Ontario, was as much a child of the American Revolution as was the United States itself. Large numbers of United Empire Loyalists had supported the crown in the War of Independence and they were not prepared to offer their allegiance to the new administration. Various resettlement schemes were proposed, including shipment to New South Wales, but the great majority chose to emigrate north and west into Canada. In 1783 ten thousand such loyalists settled along the northern shores of Lake Ontario, a ready-made community that was able to draw on its American pioneering experience and rough it for several winters in the squalid and extreme conditions of the Canadian backwoods before winning back some of its former prosperity. Over the next two decades other settlers from America joined them until the hostilities of the Anglo-American war of 1812 cut off the flow. Thereafter, strenuous efforts were made to Anglicize Upper Canada by encouraging direct emigration from Britain. Generous land grants were offered to such military gentlemen as Mrs Susanna Moodie's husband in the hope that this would create a local 'squirearchy' along English lines. Almost exactly a century later a very similar government plan, known as the Soldier-Settler Scheme, brought ex-army officers out to East Africa in the early 1920s. They, too, had to build up their homesteads from scratch but with the considerable advantage – at least, in the short term – of being able to draw on a local native work force. For Mrs Moodie and her friends, however, there was to be no quick escape from the harsh realities of frontier life.

Formidable barriers of communication had to be overcome by these early settlers in the Canadian wilderness. It took twelve days to cover the 120-mile stretch of white water on the St Lawrence between Montreal and Prescott, where passengers had to transfer to sailing ships for the journey across to Lake Ontario. If their holdings were not accessible by water then 'corduroy' timber roads might have to be laid over what was often marshy or muddy ground. Before crops could be planted or houses raised, the land itself had to be cleared, and since subsistence farming was the order of the day, good housing and household niceties came a long way down the list of priorities. In the face of such grinding 'severe duty', social standing went by the board.

An illustration from *The British Farmer's Guide to Ontario*, published in 1848, shows a typical Upper Canadian home-stead in the process of transition from the first-stage pioneer log cabin, built with felled timber from the cleared land, to the modest frame-construction farmhouse with clapboard walls that signalled the approach of prosperity. A notable feature of this hard pioneering life is the growth of an equally strong communal spirit among farmers, which found expression in co-operative exercises known as 'bees', when neighbours got together to help with harvesting or to build one another's barns – meetings that were frequently topped with barn dances and the consumption of locally distilled whisky. The local settlement, often made up of no more than a general store, a tavern-cum-hotel, a smithy-cum-livery and perhaps a corn mill, assumed additional significance as a social centre in a still hostile landscape that lacked other amenities.

A similar pattern of up-country settlement could have been observed getting under way in Australia at this time, but here built around the twin figures of the 'squatter' and his merino sheep. Australia's role as an 'extensive gaol to the empire' had not prevented free settlers from setting up smallholdings on the coastal strip near Sydney, but the land was proving to be more than a match for the small settler and the peasant farmer. It needed the enterprise of men like John Macarthur, who introduced the Spanish merino to Australia and proved its worth, to demonstrate that Australia's future lay with the sheep-farmer and the land-owner. The crossing of the Blue Mountain Range in 1813, followed by the discovery of the 'Australia Felix' country south of the Murray a decade later, opened up many thousands of acres of open grassland to those who had not only courage and foresight but also the necessary capital to establish themselves as graziers and squatters – or to employ convict 'ticket of leave' men to squat on their behalf. When the first commercial export of Australian wool was made in 1821 a mere 175,000 tons were sent to England. Within forty

OPPOSITE *Craigie-Longfellow House, built in 1759 by Major John Vassall, a Tory who fled in 1774. The house was subsequently used by George Washington as his headquarters.*

*Elizabeth cottage, Kingston, Ontario. Built in the mid-nineteenth century,
this is a typical example of the Gothic style,
which was becoming increasingly popular at that time.*

years New South Wales was supplying half of England's total wool imports.

It was the British middle classes who made up the bulk of these early squatters, significant numbers arriving by way of the British and Indian Armies in India, since a strong link already existed between Australia and other British dependencies in the East – a connection that played an important role in the exchange of architectural ideas and influences. These gentlemen squatters required what in middle-class terms amounted to a modest capital investment of two to three thousand pounds to get themselves started. 'They purchase the largest number of sheep which they can possibly compass', writes the author of *Land and Labour in Australia* in 1845, 'and at the same time leave sufficient to provide drays, provisions etc. They incur no expense which can by any possibility be avoided, contenting themselves with clothes, provisions, tobacco etc the same as their servants.' The more determined squatter dispensed with every comfort of civilized life, 'from wine and windows to carpets and crockery', concerning himself only with 'making the most of his capital regardless of risk and hardship, so long as they lead to increased profit'.

The first squatter homes, then, were rudimentary 'slab huts' and shacks of the kind described by John Tucker, ex-convict author of the first Australian novel, *Ralph Rashleigh*, as being –

composed of the then unvarying materials of Australian architecture in the interior – slabs or thin pieces split off by means of mauls and wedges from logs, the roof covered with forest box or stringy-bark, which was stripped from the living trees in sheets of about six feet long and from two to four feet wide, laid upon rafters composed of small sapling poles just as they came out of the bush. The sheets of bark, having hoops pierced through each in pairs, were then tied on the rafters with cords twisted off the inner rind of the kurrajong tree. The whole framing of the roof was secured as it was needed by wooden pins in order to save the expense of nails.

Chinks in these slab walls were stopped up with a plaster made of cowdung and sand and the walls whitewashed with lime. Slabs and sheets of bark also provided sleeping berths and tables. Strips of calico or sailcloth, sewn together and stiffened with whitewash, served as ceilings.

These crude dwellings can still be found in the more distant corners of the Australian outback, but they represent no more than the first ripple of civilization as it continued to extend into the interior. Once profitability had been assured and capital returns began to accumulate, such slab huts were quickly replaced with more solid and consciously comfortable dwellings, of which Elizabeth Farm House, overlooking the Parramatta River near Sydney, provides the earliest surviving example. Built in 1794 for the formidable Captain John Macarthur, this is a rectangular single-storey dwelling made up of four rooms on either side of a central entrance hall. The walls are of brick, supporting a hipped roof of swamp-oak shingles with extended eaves wide enough to cover a small verandah on the eastern side of the house – a feature that appears to have been derived from the Indian bungalow but which could well have evolved locally as a logical answer to the Australian climate. Another characteristically Indian feature at Elizabeth Farm House is the location of the kitchen, along with the laundry, meat house and servants' quarters, in a separate building at the back, but this too could well be the architect's response to the social gulf that in Australia, just as much as in India, divided the 'haves' from the 'have nots'.

From this practical but elegant prototype there evolved in the 1820s and 1830s the professionally planned and built 'Australian Regency' country houses of Tasmania and New South Wales that reflected the growing self-assurance of the 'wool-growing oligarchs' of Australia. They were two-storey homes set in landscaped park-like grounds, part-English and part-Australian, with such imported refinements as marble fireplaces and doors with mortice locks and recessed butt hinges, but also tempered to the climate, with Indian mats on the floors in place of carpets, calico and sailcloth false ceilings, gaps between walls and roof to aid the circulation of air and, most obvious of all, verandahs that often extended round all four sides of the building, supported on turned wooden columns with criss-cross timber railings. A similar admixture of styles was apparent in the

*Drayton, near Charleston, South Carolina, 1738–42. This elegant mansion
was probably designed by its builder, John Drayton,
and was the first Anglo-Palladian house in the United States.*

Vaucluse House, Sydney, built for William Charles Wentworth,
the 'Father of the Australian Constitution'
in the early nineteenth century.

gardens that now surrounded such country homes, laid out in the English manner but more often than not approached along shady avenues of eucalyptus. Other typically Australian innovations introduced in later years included outer wallings of brick to hide inner timber walls, double-leafed stone walls with empty cavities and, to avoid white ants, the building of bungalows on piles raised two or three feet off the ground, which also allowed air to circulate freely underneath.

Nowhere were the ideals of this aristocracy of working gentlemen and their equally hard-working ladies (so hard-working, it seems, that they abandoned the British middle-class custom of afternoon tea for the working-class custom of an early supper) given clearer expression than at Camden Park, built for the Macarthur family in 1834 by a failed

Mount Pleasant, near Launceston, Tasmania,
a private house, built c 1870.

English architect. A Scotsman who visited Camden Park a few years later noted that he had never seen 'a more agreeable English-looking place. The house, the park, the water, the gardens, the style of everything and every person, master and servants, resembled so much what one meets with in the old country, that I could scarcely believe myself sixteen thousand miles from it.' From such beginnings Australia developed a sturdy Georgian Palladian revival architecture that was applied, in true Palladian manner, principally to the rural requirements of a sheep-farming economy. It was a pragmatic Palladianism, by which the wealthy sheep-farmers emulated their English country cousins by building up the homesteads of their often vast and isolated sheep stations after the manner of British landed gentry, but with a range of adaptations that matched the climate. Even during the period of Victorian eclecticism that characterized the latter half of the nineteenth century, Australian country architecture never lost its head or its sense of practicality. That touch of 'severe duty' remained, even though the occupants could now

The chapel at Mount Pleasant, Tasmania
(see previous page).

Georgian terrace, Camden, New South Wales.

Intricate iron-work gives distinction to this private house
above Watson's Bay, Sydney, built in the mid-nineteenth century.

*Abercrombie, near Orange, New South Wales. The design is
a late nineteenth-century copy of a Dumfriesshire hunting lodge
belonging to the Duke of Buccleuch of the time.*

enjoy the 'refinement and luxuries' that their forebears had eschewed. When the writer Anthony Trollope visited Australia in 1873 the Squatting Age was long since over in New South Wales but was still being enacted in Western Australia. However, the ascendancy of the 'wool-growing oligarchs' was undiminished:

The number of sheep will generally indicate with fair accuracy the mode of life at the head station: 100,000 sheep and upwards require a professed man-cook and a butler to look after them; 40,000 sheep cannot be shorn without a piano; 20,000 is the lowest number that renders napkins at dinner imperative; 10,000 require absolute plenty, meat in plenty, tea in plenty, brandy and water and colonial wine in plenty but do not expect champagne, sherry or made dishes, and you are supposed to be content with continued mutton or continued beef – as the squatter may at the time be in the way of killing sheep or oxen.

The same agreeable mixture of old country traditions tempered to accommodate local climate and local building materials can be seen further east in New Zealand, where some of the earliest surviving homes were put up by the missionary societies, who built (as did the Puritans) to last. Kemp House, at Kerikeri on North Island, built by a shipwright named William Hall for the Christian Missionary Society in 1821, is a wooden-framed two-storey building with a central stairwell and a verandah on two sides. Elegant and unpretentious, it was, in the words of a contemporary, 'finished in a superior manner to the wooden houses of Hampstead'. Constructed a decade later, Wianate

56

North Mission House on South Island is even more consciously antipodean: a double-roofed bungalow entirely surrounded by a verandah, drawing its inspiration from the Anglo-Indian bungalow by way of New South Wales. This Australian connection was, inevitably, a very strong one, and the relatively advanced state of building there by comparison with still underpopulated New Zealand, where there were scarcely 35,000 colonists in the middle of the nineteenth century, provided plenty of work for Australian architects and builders, including the export of pre-fabricated houses built in Sydney and shipped across to Wellington and Auckland.

The 1840s and 1850s saw increasing uniformity as buildings began to spread throughout the colonies. Newly published manuals, such as Nicholson's *New Practical Builder and Workman's Companion*, became the *vade mecum* of every settler – and these settlers themselves became increasingly numerous. Approximately three million people are believed to have emigrated from Britain and Ireland during the second quarter of the century. The great majority went to the United States and Canada, but from 1831 onwards the introduction of assisted passages brought out increasing numbers of Britain's 'redundant poor' to Australia and New Zealand. However, the democratization of these two colonies really begins with the discovery of the copper and silver-lead fields of the 1840s, and of gold in New South Wales and Victoria in 1851. The astonishing scale of the 1851-3 gold rushes in Victoria can be judged by the way in which its population swelled from 70,000 in 1850 to 333,000 in 1855. Within a decade the state's annual expenditure on roads and bridges rose from a paltry £11,000 to an astonishing £3,163,000, much of which went on the urbanization of Melbourne, to the point where it rivalled Sydney and housed over forty per cent of Victoria's population.

Like other new arrivals, the 'diggers' who flooded into Australia in the 1850s started out by living rough, either under canvas in such tented encampments as Canvas Town at Emerald Hill or under bark and rough-hewn slabs like the early squatters. Their needs for more durable housing were answered by the introduction – by goldminers from California, so it is said – of the cheap and easily erected pre-fabricated cottage, shipped over from America and Singapore in numbered parts to be erected on site. The mass-produced softwood timber-frame cottage with clapper-board walls was soon providing the background for the first photographs of outback and up-country settlements, not only in Australia but as far afield as Clinton, British Columbia and Whitianga, Mercury Bay, New Zealand.

The arrival of galvanized corrugated iron sheeting completed the process by which popular housing became available to all classes of colonial society. The result was that a drab and nondescript uniformity, which had hitherto been confined to the towns and larger settlements, was introduced to the colonial countryside, a conformity of style that paid scant regard either to local customs or to local materials. Ironically, this standardization united the furthest corners of that much-vaunted Empire upon which the proverbial sun never set in a way that its founders could neither have imagined nor desired.

British colonial expansion did not, of course, occur in a vacuum, yet it is a fact that in North America, Australia and New Zealand the presence of a native population failed to influence to any significant degree the manner in which the settlers went about erecting their homes – except perhaps in the raising of stockades or forts when danger threatened. Where the local population did radically affect and influence the social behaviour of the British, however, was in India and, to a lesser extent, in British south-east Asia. In both these regions a two-way traffic in ideas was to result in the richest and most clearly articulated style of colonial architecture and living in the British Empire, one that was to spread far beyond the territorial confines of south and south-east Asia. The natural outcome of this architectural cross-fertilization was the bungalow, while in terms of social organization it produced the phenomenon of the civil and military station. Both are key features of British colonial architecture and deserve detailed examination.

The word 'bungalow', so rich in connotations both tropical and suburban in British usage, has been defined in

*Corrugated iron became the essential roofing material
in Australia but its use was rarely taken to this extreme.*

the Anglo-Indian glossary known as *Hobson-Jobson* as a building 'of one storey and covered by a pyramidal roof, which in the normal bungalow is of thatch but may be of tiles'. In both name and form it has its origins in the old Hindu kingdom of Bangala (later redefined by the British as the Bengal Presidency) through which the East India Company first gained access to the hinterland, or *mofussil*, of the 'ceded and conquered provinces of Upper Hindoostan' in the second half of the eighteenth century. 'Even Englishmen live in what are really stationary tents which have run aground on low brick platforms', writes a young district official newly appointed to an outlying corner of Bengal in 1801. 'They are "bungalows", a word I know not how to render unless by a Cottage. These are always thatched with straw on the roof and the walls are sometimes of bricks and often of mats. To hide the sloping roofs we put up a kind of artificial ceiling made of white cloth.'

It was this simple bungalow, 'taken up by the first settlers in Bengal from the native style of edifice', according to a writer in the *Saturday Review* in 1886, that was 'thence

carried to other parts of India' after being 'materially improved'. The same writer explains that 'in Bengal and notably in the districts near Calcutta native houses to this day are divided into *ath-chala*, *chau-chala* and *Bangala*, or eight-roofed, four-roofed and Bengali or common huts'. The *ath-chala* house he describes as having a roof with 'four distinct sides with four more projections, so as to cover a verandah all round the house, which is square', compared with the more straightforward four-sided and two-sided roofs of the *chau-chala* and *Bangala* huts.

Doubts have been cast on the Indian origins of the bungalow, one theory tracing it back to the Palladian-style 'garden houses' that the wealthier nabobs and senior European officials had built for themselves in the suburbs of the presidency towns. Many were impressive buildings indeed, among them those that lined the banks of the Hoogly at Garden Reach below Calcutta and excited the admiration and envy of new arrivals to the city, such as the eponymous hero of Charles D'Oyly's poem *Tom Raw* in 1828:

Bungalow at Hyderabad, early nineteenth century. It served, as it still does, as vicarage to St George's Church, Hyderabad.

The Garden Reach – Oh! what a lovely reach.
Fit suburb of a city so renowned,
The eye pursues its bright enamelled beach,
With airy villas fancifully crowned.

However, it is hard to see how such stately mansions, two-storey and vertical in emphasis, modified though many were to take on verandahs with Tuscan colonnades, could have been cut down into the more modest and – for the most part – single-storey bungalows that were to become such a dominant feature of the Anglo-Indian landscape. Certainly, the Europeans in India never had any doubts as to the local origins of the bungalow, which chroniclers of the *mofussil* scene in the formative pre-Mutiny years, such as the spirited Fanny Parkes, usually divided into two distinct types: 'If a house has a flat roof covered with flag-stones and mortar it is called a *pukka* house. If the roof be raised and it be thatched it is called a *bungalow*.'

A contemporary of Fanny Parkes was the anonymous author (describing himself simply as 'An Artist in India') of *An Anglo-Indian Domestic Sketch*, published in 1849, who also speaks of two kinds of standard dwelling. 'The form and arrangement of an English residence evidently owe their origin to the bungalow of the middling classes of natives', he writes. 'To these the bungalows of military officers and others in the *moofussul* [*sic*] are more clearly and directly attributable.' The simplest of these *mofussil* bungalows were self-evidently based on the *chau-chala* and *Bangala* peasant huts of rural Bengal. 'The thatched roof, extending considerably over all sides, is supported at the extreme edges upon bamboo wooden pillars, thus forming a covered verandah round the building', writes An Artist in India, providing explanatory drawings of both prototype and production models. 'The European resident, improving upon this, encloses the verandah by erecting either a mat or brick wall, and throwing partitions across the corner converts the verandah into little rooms. Rude as they may appear, these semi-rustic tenements are often not only pretty but very comfortable, their thick straw roofs and airy locality rendering them cool habitations.'

Enlarged to accommodate the bigger rooms demanded by Europeans, this form of country or *kutcha* (raw, unfinished) bungalow was able to provide first-stage accommodation for Europeans as they moved up-country, not only in India but also in tropical outposts as far afield as Fiji and Kenya. Indeed, with shingles or tiles replacing the thatch and with only minor modifications, the same structure could be found gracing homesteads in Australia and New Zealand.

The more complex 'eight-sided' *ath-chala* Bengali house was similarly adapted to provide homes for Europeans in the *mofussil* that were different from the other more basic *kutcha* bungalow only in outline. Here a section of masonry wall, often no more than a foot or two in height and set with windows or vents, formed a dividing line between the central upper roof and the surrounding verandah roof. Internally, however, there was very little difference between these two varieties of *kutcha* bungalow. The anonymous authoress of *Indian Outfits and Establishments* (she describes herself simply as 'An Anglo-Indian Lady') helpfully provides a ground plan of what was in 1885 still the basic, standardized up-country bungalow: a building that was square in shape and entirely surrounded by verandahs that are partially closed by four small *godowns* (store-rooms) at the four corners. An enormous drawing room, backed by a dining room, fills the central portion of the plan, with doors on either side leading out from four bedroom suites, each complete with dressing room and bathroom. There is no place in this scheme of things for a kitchen or servants' quarters. 'The huts of the native servants should never be too near', warns the anonymous authoress. 'As a rule, no native servants – not even the ayahs – sleep in the bungalow, but out in their own houses in the compound, often scarcely within call.'

Where the complications begin is over the provenance of the *pukka* (mature, finished) bungalow that replaced the *kutcha* as a second-stage dwelling. The author of *An Anglo-Indian Domestic Sketch* appears to associate this more sophisticated model with town rather than country living, which would be perfectly logical. He states that in Calcutta in 1848 there were 11,215 'dwelling-houses' of which 6,376 were upper-roomed' (two-storey) and the remainder 'lower-roomed'. The accompanying drawing shows one such single-storey bungalow, described as 'not only highly characteristic of its class but of Anglo-Indian residences in general'. Like its *kutcha* cousin, this *pukka* bungalow has a square ground plan but has been given the Neo-Classical treatment. It has a pillared porch at the front, and what should be the surrounding verandah has now been all but bricked up, even though there are arched openings at the front and windows topped by pediments at the sides. The most crucial difference between the two forms, however, lies in their roofs, for here in the *pukka* building the dominant pitched roof has been replaced by what appears at first sight to be a flat roof, very much in accordance with Fanny Parkes' definition of a *pukka* house. Flat-roofed dwellings surmounted by low walls are very much a feature of the drier regions of northern India, first penetrated by the British in the early decades of the nineteenth century. But there are excellent grounds for supposing that, in the case of the European bungalow described here, a low-pitched roof still survives but because it is set so far back it is no longer visible from the ground. The great majority of what might now be termed classical Indian bungalows of the nineteenth and twentieth centuries do indeed have such low-pitched roofs above the central portion of the house – and it is this often unseen central roof, providing the central core of the dwelling with its distinctive high ceilings and extra light and ventilation, that most clearly associates the *pukka* single-storey bungalow with what must surely have been its original model, the *ath-chala* of Bengal – even if the lower sloping roofs over the *ath-chala's* verandahs have been lost and the upper sloping roof obscured by walls or pillared balustrades.

To confuse the issue still further, the role of what in Assam and other parts of eastern India is known as the *chung* (wooden-floored) bungalow, sometimes called the 'planter's bungalow', has also to be considered. One school of thought traces this raised bungalow back to the Straits Settlements of Penang, Malacca and Singapore and to the original model of the Malay house, often built on stilts on river banks or over water. This is plausible enough since there was plenty

A mid-nineteenth-century bungalow at Bangalore,
India. As a general rule, detail
became more elaborate as the century progressed.

The bungalow allowed almost any adaptation of ideas.
Here an arcaded verandah with vernacular influence
makes an elegant portico.

The Principal's bungalow,
Colvin Taluqdars' School, Lucknow, c *1905.*

of exchange in goods, men and ideas between India and this flourishing branch of the British East India Company's business empire. The word 'compound,' for instance, which describes the enclosed area surrounding an Anglo-Indian bungalow, together with its outhouses and gardens, is not an Indian word but is derived from the Malay *kampong* or cultivated village settlement. However, it has to be remembered that settlement in south-east Asia – with the remarkable exception of the Brooke family's Rajahdom of Sarawak – was essentially a town phenomenon. The push into the interior of the Malay peninsula did not get under way until the 1880s, with the coffee and rubber planters following a decade later, so the origins of the *chung* bungalow are almost certainly to be found in the evergreen jungles of eastern India.

Health was always a major issue in the tropics – a perfectly understandable obsession when one considers the appallingly high mortality figures of these times – and nowhere were Europeans more at risk than in the malarial jungles of Assam. Even in its sixth edition, published in

Public Works Department bungalow in Sarawak.
This was the district headquarters for the Fourth Division.

1893, Surgeon-General Sir William Moore's ever-popular *Manual of Family Medicine and Hygiene for India* continues to ascribe malaria to 'a poisonous emanation' in the air. 'Judging from its effect,' writes Dr Moore, 'malaria is mostly produced near the marshy banks of rivers, in the dense jungle, on lands subjected to periodical inundation. It is reasoned that malaria is most powerful during the hours of night or when a person sleeps ... but is supposed to be somewhat heavier than atmospheric air.' No doubt the pioneer tea-planters of the 1840s and 1850s had such considerations in mind as they cleared the secondary jungles of Upper Assam for their plantations, since they soon adapted to their own comfort the distinctive raised dwellings common to all the hill tribes of Assam, Burma and south-east Asia: a bamboo and thatch or nipah-palm structure raised six feet or more off the ground on stilts, with a covered platform at the front reached by a log notched with steps. Such a structure provides excellent ventilation and safety from monsoon floods and damp, from marauding animals and from the much-feared 'poisonous emanations' of the night air.

Taking their cue from these jungle dwellings, the planters raised their own *kutcha* bungalows on hardwood tree-trunks or on brick piles. The established bungalow floor plan remained essentially unchanged, although in a great many such *chung* bungalows the front verandahs were extended forward to form wide platforms that became the main sitting room, while at the same time providing cover for a porch underneath. This covered area under the bungalow was, of course, put to good use for storage and for the parking of carriages and carts. One problem that presented itself with such bungalows was the question of servants' access from the rear, and one popular solution was to drop the bathroom down to ground level, so cutting out the necessity of having to carry water upstairs to provide baths. In some instances dining rooms were also relegated to ground level, with the end result that it became difficult to determine whether such buildings were in fact enlarged *chung* bungalows or the more solid, mansion-like two-storey *pukka* bungalows that became increasingly popular as station dwellings for *burra sahibs* in the last decades of the nineteenth century, both in India and elsewhere in the tropics.

A prominent figure in planting circles in India for over half a century was Kenneth Warren, who first went out to Assam in 1906. In a privately printed autobiography, *Tea Tales of Assam* (1975), he provides a lively account of life in these *chung* bungalows:

Bungalows in those days were all built on *chungs*, about eight to nine feet above ground, with *nahur* [very hard wood] supporting posts and an entirely timber framework and a thatch roof. The walls were in wooden panels filled in with *ekra* [reed] and plastered with *mutty* [earth] mixed with cow-dung and then covered with white lime-wash. The ceilings of the rooms were hessian cloth, also whitewashed. The space between the ceiling cloth and the thatch roof was the home of bats and occasionally snakes. My furniture consisted of my bed, which I had bought in Calcutta, and two chairs bought in the local bazaar, the rest consisted of tea-boxes inverted serving as a table, and six tea-boxes standing up sideways used as a chest of drawers or wardrobe.

The bathroom was approached by a ladder through a trap door in the bedroom floor and 'owing to the number of bats inhabiting most bungalow roofs, it was advisable to take an old tennis racquet down with you to the bathroom to keep them from sharing the bath, as they seemed to take a delight in splashing into the water as they flew around your head'. Warren also recalls how on one occasion during the rainy season he returned from his work in the heat of the day to have a cold bath: 'As I settled down in the cool of the water I felt the bath tub moving and on looking over the edge saw a large python snake slowly unwinding itself from round my tin bath, which had sloping sides under which he had been sleeping.' It is worth noting that with only minor variations Kenneth Warren's experiences were being shared at this time by teak-extractors in Burma, rubber-planters in Malaya and tea-planters in Ceylon, all areas where the *chung* bungalow was the most common form of up-country European bungalow.

Because it had almost two full centuries to develop – as compared to a maximum of seventy to eighty years in such

Tea estate bungalow, Ceylon c 1875–80.

territories as Uganda or Kenya – Anglo-Indian culture had a solidarity to it that was unmatched in any other part of the Empire. This stemmed from the fact that the civil and military personnel and their families, who outside the three presidency towns made up the European population almost in its entirety, were an extremely isolated ruling minority. They came from the same narrow background, becoming increasingly 'Anglo-Indian' with each generation as sons followed fathers or uncles into Indian service and went on to marry the daughters of other Anglo-Indians. They increasingly lost touch with their peers in British society and at the same time they became increasingly aloof from the native population, partly because their success as a ruling race created notions of racial superiority, partly as a reaction to the constant threat of absorption into a strong native culture – the fear of 'going native'. Such factors inevitably combined to make them conservative in their thinking and resistant to change, so that there is a sense of timelessness about much of British India. Order and conformity were reflected as much in its architecture as in everything else, in the way, for instance, that one PWD building, whether it be a *dak* bungalow or a Forest Officers' Rest House or a Class Three Graded Officers' bungalow (as set out in the official Warrant of Precedence), matched another, even though they might be five hundred miles and fifty years apart. And because British India so often set the tone for other colonial territories between the Tropics of Cancer and Capricorn, from the Gambia to the Gilbert and Ellice Islands, it was possible to find not only the Indian Penal Code being applied many thousands of miles outside India but also Indian rules and manuals of instruction governing sanitation, drainage and public buildings.

Order and conformity ensured the security that was so important to this isolated and caste-conscious ruling elite. Here, as in no other territory, it was 'severe duty' first and last, with the 'refinement and luxuries of European Society' being postponed until retirement and a return to Britain came along. This attitude of almost puritanical self-righteousness was wickedly mocked by William Thackeray in his famous remark in *Vanity Fair* about the contrast between life in the plains and life in the summer hill stations – 'duty and red tape; picnics and adultery'. Such hill stations – Ootacamund in the south, Shillong and Darjeeling in the east, Mount Abu in Rajasthan, Murree, Lansdowne, Simla, Mussoorie and Naini Tal in the north – provided a very necessary safety valve for the British in India, which is reflected in the deliberately un-Indian, suburban Englishness of their cottages-for-hire and their Gothic hotels – marred only by the widespread use of corrugated iron for roofing.

Order and conformity, coupled with the need for security, also lay at the heart of the civil and military station, which was a necessary prerequisite to administration and which in India developed its own style to a remarkable degree. Nowhere have its chief characteristics been better illustrated and dissected than in George Atkinson's celebrated mid-nineteenth-century Anglo-Indian satire *Curry and Rice on Forty Plates, or The Ingredients of Social Life at 'Our Station' in India*. The first plate shows the dusty mall of the fictitious civil and military station at Kabob, a small and unlovely district headquarters 'in the plains of Dekchy, in the province of Bobarchy'. The station is made up for the most part of 'mud-built edifices of whitewash and thatch', all neatly laid out in accordance with the governing principles of the day. Lying on its western extremity is the native bazaar, the 'most highly peopled quarter', whose only European denizen is a zealous German missionary. Separating the bazaar from the rest of the station is a *maidan* or open stretch of ground known as the Parade, whereon 'our dusky Trojans learn the art of war'. These native troops occupy the

OVERLEAF *Meerut Cantonment Bank, Uttar Pradesh, c 1880*
Local opinion holds that it was purpose-built,
but it is certainly domestic in style.

area to the east of the parade-ground in 'Lines' – rows of 'mud wall tenements lined with thatch'. Next to them are the quarters of their officers, also laid out in lines but with 'each dwelling, commonly called a bungalow, in its own particular territory' and built 'like exaggerated bee-hives perched on mile-stones'. Then comes a 'square whitewashed edifice with an excrescence at one end, looking for all the world like an extinguisher on a three-dozen chest' – the station church – and, close at hand, the assembly room and theatre, the station hospital, the racquets court, the band-stand and, surprisingly, the station bath, all of which combine to make up the social centre of the station, 'where the live splendour of Kabob resort when shades of evening close upon us'.

Now the Military Cantonment (pronounced 'cantoon-ment' for no known reason, since the word derives not from China but from France, as the sub-division of a town district) gives way to the Civil Lines. It passes the 'well-stocked burial ground' to one side and on the other the barracks of a British Army artillery battery, outside which is a British-owned store selling British goods – 'anything from a baby's bottle to a bolster'. Then come the Civil Lines themselves, where 'we plunge into territory that is under civil sway'. First there are government offices, 'flat-roofed edifices in the Brummagen Tuscan order, all pillars, plaster and pea-green paint', comprising, in this instance, the courts of law and the treasury. Next is the obligatory *bagh* or small park, here represented by a nascent botanical garden and on either side the 'wide-verandahed habitations of the civilians', by which the author means Britons in government employ. A second bazaar marks the outer limits of the station and completes the picture.

All that is lacking is the masonic lodge, which first made its appearance in the Indian up-country station in the third decade of the nineteenth century. In the fast-growing military station of Cawnpore, for instance, Lodge Harmony was formed in 1834 at the petition of a group of non-commissioned officers and other ranks. Such lodges were solid and unpretentious buildings, for the most part, known to the local native population as *jadu ghars* or 'houses of magic' on account of the curious and secretive rituals performed therein (just as churches in India were often referred to as *bhut khannas* or 'ghost houses'). According to Rudyard Kipling, an enthusiastic freemason in his younger days, this masculine cult transcended all races, castes and sects in what was an acutely race- and caste-conscious society. He himself was admitted at an early age to Lodge Hope and Perseverance in Lahore in 1885: 'I was entered by a Brahmo Somaj (Hindu), passed by a Mohammedan, and raised by an Englishman. My tyler was an Indian Jew.' Indeed, it was said that the masonic building in Cawnpore cantonment only survived the holocaust of the 1857 Mutiny at the express orders of the leader of the rebel forces, Nana Saheb of Bithor, who was himself a member of the lodge.

Curry and Rice was published in 1858, the year in which British sovereignty was first proclaimed over the whole of the Indian subcontinent. The form of the station that Atkinson describes had then already been in existence for half a century and more. The key to its layout lies in the word 'lines', which betrays its essentially military origin in the days of campaigning, when a military force pitched its tents and organized its forces in defensive lines, well away from the enemy (here represented by the 'native quarter' or bazaar) with a clear field of fire (the *maidan* or parade ground). First came the tents of the Indian troops, then those of their officers, followed by military headquarters, the supporting British troops and finally the civilian camp followers. Very few stations reflect this defensive plan to the letter but the main elements – separation from the native town, the intervening *maidan*, the military lines and then the civil lines – were nearly always present. This may seem isolationist to us now but it should be remembered that in India older towns were often abandoned when over-building, encroachments and sanitary conditions made them all but uninhabitable. Segregation by caste, family traditions that led to several generations crowding into one dwelling, and the widespread lapse of sound local government in the pre-British period had all contributed to a decline in standards in Indian urban life. The British response, motivated quite as much by fears for their health as for their safety, was to lay out their own independent colonies in the countryside. In *Leaves from a Diary* (1896) a retired government official named B.L. Clay describes Chittagong, one of the oldest stations in Bengal and the site of an East India company trading factory, as he first knew it in 1863:

The native quarter and bazaars were mostly hidden by trees. There was no regular *maidan* but in front of the regimental lines was a grassy stretch, clear of scrub which served as a parade and recreation ground. Here too was Scandal Corner, a small bridge at the junction of four cross-roads. The station possessed a racquet-court, billiard table, and swimming-bath, not a regular covered-in place but a bamboo bathing hut on piles in one corner of a pretty little lake. The Church stood near the Collectorate, a good-sized building with a square tower and stained glass window. Most of the houses were one-storeyed, with flat roofs and thatched verandahs; government buildings and some of the large private houses were *pukka* throughout, or nearly so. There were *kutcha* bungalows also, buildings of timber and bamboo matting with thatched roofs.

The European population of the station at Chittagong then comprised eight covenanted civil servants, three police officers, a civil surgeon, a collector of customs and five military officers. There were no European non-officials.

By the time that Chittagong had ceased to be an up-country station and had become a bustling port, a great many other civil stations had been laid out: Kuala Lumpur, for instance, was being cut out of the secondary jungle beside a Chinese tin-mining settlement at the junction of the Klang and Gombak rivers by Frank Swettenham and other Straits Settlements 'thrusters' in the early 1880s; British Kampala was being staked out under the barrel of a Maxim gun by the British Imperial East Africa Company's chief trouble-shooter, Frederick Lugard, a decade later. At Kuala Lumpur the police lines look down across the open space of the *padang* at the Chinese village beyond, and are in turn looked down upon by the bungalows of the government officers to the south and those of the European traders to the north. However, dominating the *padang* is a complex of

Selangor Club, Kuala Lumpur, Malaysia, known as the 'Spotted Dog'.
Mock Tudor was very popular in the late Empire.

mock-Tudor bungalows that represents a new feature on the station map. It is the station club, in Kuala Lumpur known as the Selangor Club, otherwise called the 'Dog' or 'Spotted Dog', founded in 1884 and the oldest such institution in the Malay States.

One of the most striking features of the British middle classes overseas is their almost obsessive interest in games and sporting pursuits, often undertaken in the interests of good health, out of which there developed tent clubs, gymkhana clubs and station clubs that became centres not only for sports but also for drinking and relaxation.

Aesthetically and architecturally they were rarely impressive, and in the more remote corners often consisted of nothing more than a wooden shack with a tin or thatch roof, a bar in one corner and a billiard table in another, but they provided an invaluable service in strengthening the cohesiveness that was a necessary part of running an empire and bolstering the mores and the morale of the British expatriate community. The club made the station complete. It was a place where the cares and worries of 'severe duty' could be temporarily shelved while the delights of 'the refinement and luxuries of European Society' were savoured.

71

The Club, Ootacamund. Built as a hotel for Sir William Rumbold in 1830,
it was taken over in 1843 and was to become one of the most prestigious clubs in India.
It was here that Neville Chamberlain invented snooker.

*Adyar Club, Madras, early nineteenth century. In essence this a typical
Madras 'flat top' garden house, but the octagonal cupola
is an unusual departure from the stereotype.*

Existential Cities

Gillian Tindall

'Cities simply cannot be "explained" by their locations or other given sources', writes Jane Jacobs in *The Economy of Cities* (1970). 'Their existence as cities and the sources of their growth lie within themselves, in the processes and growth systems that go on within them. Cities are not ordained, they are wholly existential.'

This is not the approach favoured by traditional geography, which enshrines a *post hoc* fallacy in such assertions as that this great city 'owes its existence' to a river estuary or that one to a well-drained upland. In practice, as Jane Jacobs demonstrates, for every city site there are often many other sites in the same region which, judged impartially, would be equally suitable and sometimes better, but which just happen not to have acquired a settlement on them. It is the accidents of history rather than of geography that seem largely to determine which random cluster of huts, which chance staging post, eventually grows into a world metropolis and which does not. And if this is true even of cities which are an organic and indigenous growth on the land on which they stand, it is far more true of colonial cities. Their establishment is typically arbitrary, and geographically even perverse, depending solely as it does on possession, on coincidence, on the fortunes of war. Sometimes indeed the creation of a city is an attempt to create a fact – to reinforce an otherwise shaky claim to alien soil. The colonizing power may not actually want or need a city on that particular piece of land, but they don't want anyone else to have one there, and they need this foothold in order to gain control of a wider area, or at any rate to appear to gain control. A city

can, at its inception, be an act of aggression, a public relations exercise, even a piece of quixotic hubris and folly on the part of one free-booting individual. But once it is fairly established, other forces take over, a dynamic towards growth and accretion that arises within the city itself.

Calcutta, the quintessential and largest colonial city of its era, described by Nirad Chaudhuri as 'an illegitimate child of London and Manchester', occupies a site which no sensible man would have chosen for a market town, much less for an imperial capital. In fact no choice as such was made. It was the ruffianly Job Charnock who 'founded' Calcutta more or less by accident, picking it as a monsoon stopover point in 1686 because it had a particularly large banyan tree that would provide a suitable focus and shelter for his camp. Even its name speaks of disease and death, for it derives from Kalikata, the temple there to Kali, consort of Shiva the Destroyer. Mark Twain, lecturing in Calcutta at the end of the last century, described its climate as 'enough to make a brass doorknob mushy'. Sir George Trevelyan, the writer son of an Indian Finance Minister, had already stigmatized the place a generation earlier: 'Find, if you can, a more uninviting spot than Calcutta ... It unites every condition of a perfectly unhealthy situation ... The place is so bad by nature that human efforts could do little to make it worse.' This in the 1860s, when Bombay, Calcutta's busily expanding rival, was preening herself on the fact that her mortality rate was currently lower than that of London. Bombay was confined to a rocky, sea-girt island from which malarial swamps had gradually been drained, while Cal-

The main street, Simla, leading to the Gaiety Theatre.
Without the superficial detail, it would easily fit
into a Home Counties English town.

cutta was sited on the blackish, oozing mud of a tidal estuary: naturally the occupants of Bombay had begun to suggest with increasing confidence that their own city was now more suited to the seat of government in India. Yet the sheer size of Calcutta by then, the weight of her history and the powerful forces of inertia were sufficient to keep her the capital until the deliberate construction of New Delhi. And New Delhi itself is the perfect counter-example of a colonial city that *was* planned on a chosen site, but too late, with disregard for the way the tide of events was then running; an artificial structure which only questionably qualifies as a colonial city at all. In its own eccentric way, the precipitous Simla was more successful, because better loved and more representative of the people who built it – and that developed on its rocky heights more or less by chance, since one officer built a bungalow there for the good of his health

ABOVE *The British desire to create a home from home cannot be seen more clearly than in this row of houses in Port Elizabeth, South Africa. They would pass unnoticed in any south-coast town in England.*

LEFT *Donkin Street, Port Elizabeth. The top five houses are a later addition, but the whole area round the Donkin Reserve is largely original and unaltered.*

in 1819, and two others followed suit.

Delhi was planted on the site of an older, indigenous settlement of symbolic importance. So were a number of other colonial cities: Bulawayo, in Rhodesia (now Zimbabwe), is a classic example of this. It is an industrial centre and railway junction a long way from anywhere, with no natural feature in the way of a river or mountain to provide a *raison d'être*. It is in fact on the site of the native *kraal* which was the last redoubt of Lobengula, the Chief of the Matabeles. It was deliberately founded by Rhodes in December 1893 when he had, with a body of men from Salisbury he referred to as 'bakers and butchers and men in stores and connected with business', pursued Lobengula to his retreat, sustained an ambush and a massacre, and had massacred and destroyed in turn. The town was designed on a classic grid pattern with each street wide enough to turn a

whole wagon team of oxen. It was officially 'opened' a mere six months later by Dr Jameson (he who was to figure in the Jameson Raid the following year) with words that might stand for the attitudes of early colonial settlers almost everywhere, and which Job Charnock himself would have recognized: 'It is my job, gentlemen, to declare this town open. I don't think we want any talk about it. I make this declaration now. There is plenty of whisky and soda inside [the newly built hotel], so come on in.'

Much more frequently, however, in Africa as in Australia and India, the colonial settlements which were to grow into great cities were not so much founded as perched initially on whatever toehold of land the invading Europeans had managed to gain. Sometimes it was just a spot, perhaps with some qualities as a natural harbour, where the first landfall had happened to take place. Cape Town in South Africa

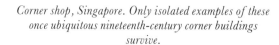

Corner shop, Singapore. Only isolated examples of these once ubiquitous nineteenth-century corner buildings survive.

and Botany Bay in New South Wales come into this category. Indeed the thriving community in Cape Town was long confined to the narrow coastal plain, and only gradually in the course of the nineteenth century pushed its way further into the mountainous area then in the possession of pastoral native tribes. (These conquering forays are described in one current South African tourist brochure as 'the Frontier Wars, which so plagued the early settlers...'!) Similarly, in Asia at an earlier date (different continents move through a near-identical cycle at different points in time), almost all the original colonial settlements were on the shore, and most typically on some promontory or semi-island, which was either what the colonizing power had managed to wrest from the native residents, or what they wanted to hang on to as a buccaneering vantage-point against their European rivals. Bombay, Calcutta, Madras, Singapore and Hong Kong come into this category. So, for that matter, does New York City.

Bombay and Surat, both on the west coast of India, form an instructive example of the non-geographic forces that have promoted the growth of one colonial settlement at the expense of another. In the early days of the Honourable East India Company (founded under licence from the crown as a trading company in 1600) the Company's main 'factory' (agency house) was at Surat, on the estuary of a river some two hundred miles to the north of Bombay. The island of Bombay (or rather the cluster of seven islands interconnected by salt swamps of which it was then composed) was acquired almost accidentally by the British crown as part of the dowry of Catharine of Braganza, the consort of Charles II (the same job-lot of Portuguese possessions included Tangiers in north Africa). Portugal, along with Holland, was then Britain's main rival in the East; the Viceroy of Goa, the chief Portuguese holding in India, was reluctant to hand over Bombay, foreseeing with remarkable

prescience that this toehold might lead step by step to an eventual take-over of the subcontinent by the British. Yet the British themselves were unimpressed by their new possession. Pepys called it 'a poor little island', and there was even talk, a few years later, of selling it back to the Portuguese. The first Governors of Bombay were only deputies: the main government remained at Surat, which, however, was not actually owned by the British, but was leased from the Mogul Emperor Aurangzeb. Had the British been able at that point to get their hands on Surat, almost certainly it would have become, and would remain today, the main metropolis of western India. (The idea recently put forward by one otherwise thoughtful commentator – Partha Mitter – that one of the reasons why Surat failed to develop as a colonial port city might have been the lack of space for gardens inside the town, is wholly fantastic.) Ths climate was much better than that of Bombay – where the early Governors and their retinues were in the habit of dying almost before they could take office – and Surat also offered a better natural harbour. Bombay is today an important port, but its original small bay offered no better protection for ships, and fewer amenities, than many of the ancient natural ports up that coast such as Supara (Ophir), Chawl and Bassein: any one of these might have been considered a more suitable place for the foundation of a colonial city than Bombay, with its poor communication with the mainland and its lack of land for growing food.

However, when the Portuguese made discreet overtures to Charles II about re-purchasing it, the East India Company stepped in and bought it themselves from the British crown to avoid losing it entirely. Then, having invested so heavily in it, they set to work almost pig-headedly to make it into a possession worth having. The first British Governor to move his residence there from Surat was Gerald Aungier,

---

OVERLEAF, LEFT *The island and city of Bombay, 1816;*
RIGHT *Bombay c 1870. Extensive landfilling and dock building*
have taken place in the intervening years.

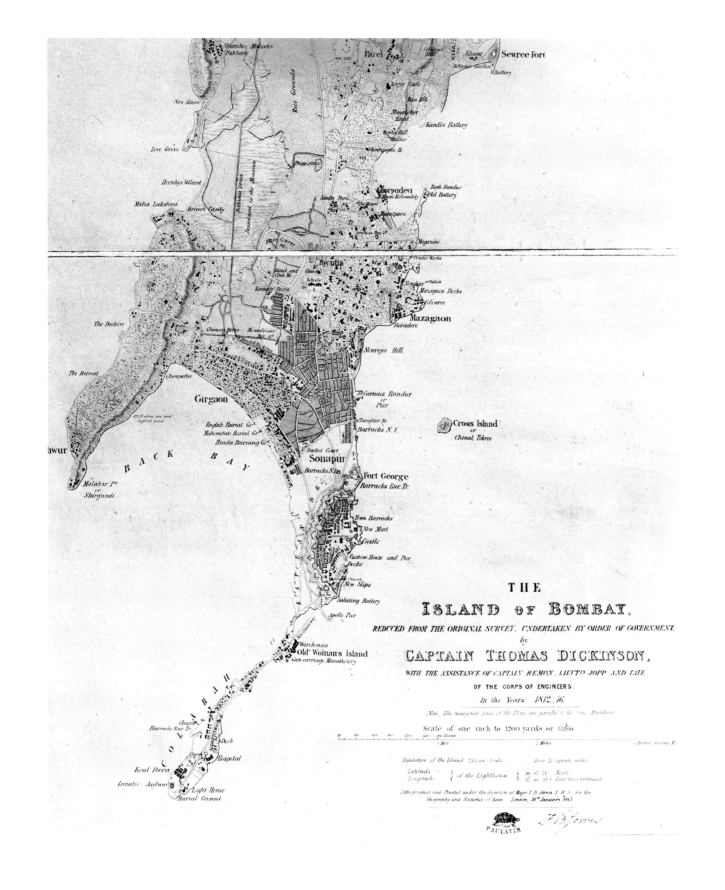

THE
ISLAND OF BOMBAY,
REDUCED FROM THE ORIGINAL SURVEY, UNDERTAKEN BY ORDER OF GOVERNMENT
by
CAPTAIN THOMAS DICKINSON,
WITH THE ASSISTANCE OF CAPTAIN REMON, LIEUT.ᵗˢ JOPP AND TATE
OF THE CORPS OF ENGINEERS.
In the Years 1812..16.

Note. The marginal lines of the Plan are parallel to the True Meridian

Scale of one inch to 1200 yards or 1/43200

Population of the Island 215,650 Souls.   Area 20 square miles.
Latitude } of the Lighthouse { 18.53.21   North
Longitude   72.46.38.7 East from Greenwich

Lithographed and Printed under the direction of Major T.B. Jervis, F.R.S. for the
Geography and Statistics of Asia. London, 31ˢᵗ January 1843.

PAULATIM

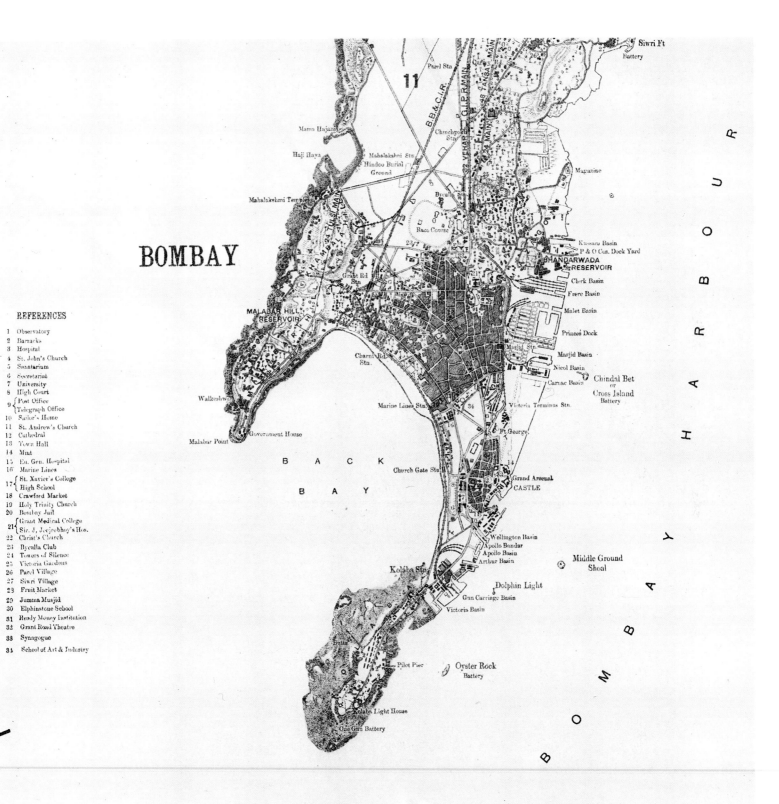

BOMBAY

REFERENCES

1 Observatory
2 Barracks
3 Hospital
4 St. John's Church
5 Sanatarium
6 Secretariat
7 University
8 High Court
9 { Post Office
   { Telegraph Office
10 Sailor's Home
11 St. Andrew's Church
12 Cathedral
13 Town Hall
14 Mint
15 En. Gen. Hospital
16 Marine Lines
17 { St. Xavier's College
    { High School
18 Crawford Market
19 Holy Trinity Church
20 Bombay Jail
21 { Grant Medical College
    { Sir J. Jeejeebhoy's Hos.
22 Christ's Church
23 Byculla Club
24 Towers of Silence
25 Victoria Gardens
26 Parel Village
27 Siwri Village
28 Fruit Market
29 Jumma Musjid
30 Elphinstone School
31 Ready Money Institution
32 Grant Road Theatre
33 Synagogue
34 School of Art & Industry

and he had visionary plans for 'the city . . . which by God's assistance is intended to be built', an empire-building settlement if ever there was one. He died, however, of the inevitable fever, before half his plans could be achieved, and the embryo city languished for another generation at least, wracked by plagues, sieges, pirates and internal dissensions, an 'unhealthful, depopulated, ruined island'. Its gradual growth and stabilization from about 1720 onwards still did not stem from any internal dynamic as much as from the continued efforts and funds of the East India Company, which worked away at building up its port and establishing ship-building yards; these were staffed mainly by skilled Parsi shipwrights invited, with inducements, from Surat. Right up to the end of the eighteenth century, the Company still debated periodically whether Bombay was worth its keep. Not until the coming of steamships in the 1830s, and the establishment of the 'overland' route to India via the Red Sea (later to be confirmed by the cutting of the Suez Canal) did Bombay really begin to grow and thrive of its own volition, but once this point had been reached, its growth proved unstoppable. Today Bombay, spreading far beyond the confines of its original island, has about eight million people (Calcutta has eleven million, but is economically stagnant), and the Bombay-Poona-Nasik triangle is the largest industrial complex in mainland Asia.

Essentially, then, the most typical early colonial settlement is a defensible trading port with, on one side, either the open sea or a wide, seaward-flowing river. The earliest British possessions in India fall into this category, as do Cape Town, Port Elizabeth, Mombasa, Lagos, and – a miniature example of the same model – Freetown, in Sierra Leone. So, come to that, do Boston, New York, Baltimore, and Philadelphia, all cities established and even to some extent developed when America was a British colony. In all these cases the main threat to the embryo settlements was intitially felt to come from competitors appearing from over the sea, which was also the main – indeed, the only – channel of communication. Headlands were mapped, islands extensively surveyed, estuaries and deltas plumbed when interiors were yet a mystery. Inland Africa long remained

'the Dark Continent'; the Indian ports were well-established as presidencies before any force daringly marched overland from one to another, 'through ways unknown and uncharted on our maps'. Therefore it was only with the passage of time that the seaboard settlers found it necessary to erect or strengthen landward defences, either because the local populations were becoming resistant to visitors from over the sea, or because the European power struggle was currently being fought out in that part of the world.

A defensible site is usually, by definition, a restricted site, and thus we have the paradox that the very qualities that make the site desirable as a place of settlement initially are also those which make it unsuitable or difficult for continued expansion. The fact that many of these fortified trading posts have expanded relentlessly nevertheless, bursting their old corsets of walls, jumping rivers, invading and colonizing unsuitable swamps, climbing up and over the inhospitable hillsides that were once their natural boundaries, is an indication of the blind, self-generative power of a thriving city once it gets into its stride.

No city can fossilize – though the dreams of town-planners persistently suggest otherwise. To maintain itself, any city must have a reason for existence in terms of economy; and change is, therefore, an inevitable concomitant of urban health. It is impossible that we should now see any of the prototype colonial cities mentioned above in their original form. Had they remained as small, as cut off and as parochial as they were, they would by now have withered away and fallen into ruin – as indeed the old Arab port of Mombasa had by the end of the nineteenth century (before it was revived as a railhead for the Kenya-Uganda Railway); or as the old Portuguese fortified town of Bassein, just up the coast from Bombay, has become – a creeper-covered relic, totally deserted. The one exception to this natural law is Williamsburg, the little township which was briefly the capital of Virginia before the American War of Independence; and indeed the 'preservation' of this colonial town-museum is almost wholly artificial. Its present-day appearance is a sign not of a genuine persistence of the past, but of the wealth of present-day America and of the important role of tourism in the economic scheme of things. 'Time has passed by old Williamsburg', in the language of the tourist brochure, but what in fact time had done to it by the early part of the twentieth century was to turn it into a decayed backwater almost indistinguishable from many others, its small eighteenth-century houses altered and defaced, or else gone altogether, mere grass-grown plots or parking lots. It is money and special interest and considerable reconstruction that have turned the town back into a simulacrum of itself in 1765, when the Stamp Act was denounced there in the Capitol building at one end of Gloucester Street, thus lighting the fuse that exploded into war.

In any case, the history of Williamsburg always ran curiously counter to the natural history of colonial settlement, for it grew not round a port or a fort but round a college of education – normally one of the later acquisitions in any settlement, part of the process of gentrification along with the museum, the club house, the tree-shaded, wealthy suburb and the municipal park. (The old 'Company gardens' that were an important adjunct to some early

Eighteenth-century street in Providence, Rhode Island.

settlements were intended as much for the growing of vegetables as for recreation.) The Williamsburg site, originally called Middle Plantation, was the one chosen under William and Mary for the erection of a college to educate the sons of planters to be gentlemen, and to train ministers to save souls. The college was built, but not without some opposition from the Lords of the Treasury in England, one of whom is reported to have said: 'Souls? Damn your souls! Make tobacco!' One hears here the authentic note of colonialist self-interest that was the pervading ethic of the East India Company themselves (they who, with their ships of tea, were to have a direct hand in provoking the War of Independence), and also of Rhodes, two hundred years later, with his bellicose troop of 'bakers and butchers and men in stores and connected with business'. Trade, not education, is always the essential business of imperialism, though at the height of her imperial power Britain maintained a sustained and convincing pretence to the contrary. Trade rather than education is, come to that, the essential business of cities – or rather, education and all that comes under the broad heading of 'culture' tends to follow only where trade is well established. The true cultural centre of colonial America was never Williamsburg but Philadelphia, the wealthiest of the cities and also the one with the most cosmopolitan intake. There, among the serviceable rowhouses of south Philadelphia and the tree-lined streets of Society Hill, the ethic and style of expansion in the New World may still be glimpsed, rather than in the self-conscious, Southern Gentleman style of Williamsburg.

Overall, Philadelphia, like Boston and New York, like the big Indian cities, like Melbourne, Kingston, and numerous others around the world, would be unrecognizable today to its early inhabitants on account of its sheer size. Some old-established cities had achieved a metropolitan extent and appearance by the late nineteenth century. Calcutta was, to

Kipling's eyes, by then 'many-sided, smokey, and magnificent', even as London was – 'We have left India behind us at Howrah Bridge, and now we enter foreign parts. No, not wholly foreign. Say, rather, too familiar.' (*The City of Dreadful Night*, 1891.) We may note in passing that then, as today, for a city to become larger and more modern was synonymous with its becoming more 'westernized' – an awkward existential fact which even the current rise of Islamic consciousness is failing to abolish. But to most cities, including colonial ones, spectacular growth has only come well within this century. Indeed, to examine city plans dating from before the First World War and then to compare them with more up-to-date examples is, in many cases, to see the notorious rise in world population graphically expressed before your eyes.

In 1800 there were only twenty-two cities in the world with a population of more than one hundred thousand people, and all of them were in Europe. By 1900 there were a hundred and sixty cities of this size worldwide, and nineteen with a population approaching one million or more, including London with four million, New York with two-and-a-half million, and Moscow, Bombay, Calcutta, and Rio de Janeiro all with close on a million. By 1950 there were seventy-five cities in the world with a population of a million or more; in 1960 there were a hundred and forty-one; and in 1975 there were a hundred and ninety-one. The estimated figure for 1986 is that there will be two hundred and seventy-three – most of them, of course, not so much 'cities' in the traditional sense of the word as huge, sprawling, amorphous metropolitan areas. The largest agglomeration is Tokyo; the next largest is thought to be Mexico City. The latter is outside the scope of this book, but it is in certain ways a quintessential colonial city in that it was originally built on a defensible island in the middle of a lake, on the destroyed remains of a conquered settlement. Today the

---

OPPOSITE *Two original buildings dating from the early part of this century in Kuala Lumpur. Modern development threatens most areas such as this.*

84

lake is full of the city – but the city is also full of the lake, for everything subsides into the imperfectly drained soil.

Comparable in some ways is Lagos, the capital of Nigeria. It was built on an island within a lagoon, and settled in the nineteenth century by freed slaves from Sierra Leone and then by Afro-Brazilians. The Brazilian element conveyed to the town a Hispanic style of architecture, much of it now destroyed, but the British Government annexed the place in 1861. The island is five miles long and nowhere is it more than two miles wide. Already in 1954, a long time ago in terms of Third World city growth, a British visitor, Elspeth Huxley, was describing the place in these terms: 'Lagos assaults you with its squalor and vitality. The narrow streets, the houses – hovels, mainly – made of mud or old tin, and packed close as playing cards, the stinking open drains, the noise, the traffic, the jostling throngs – Lagos is eastern in its feeling that there sheer, naked human life, mere existence, bubbles and pullulates with the frightening fecundity of bacteria' (*Four Guineas*). Yet at this date the city had barely a million people. Today it has an estimated five-and-a-half million, and, at half a million more than Cairo, is the largest city in Africa. The original island is half business section, half an exclusive residential area. The rest of the city has poured over three hopelessly congested bridges on to the mainland, but here the pressure on space is no less. One-time family houses have become crammed lodging houses, their gardens full of corrugated iron shacks. The city is in the stranglehold of its own success. A population of fifteen million is projected for the end of this century.

Other, more fortunate cities have grown considerably but have either not had the same geographic pressures on them or have somehow been able to resolve their problems around the physical obstacles. Cape Town, for example, has been able to retain its original form, and much of its beauty, by the presence of the Lion's Head hill sitting squarely in the way of central expansion, backed by Table Mountain, while wealthy commuter suburbs have been able to snake off along the shores and up the valley to the western side. Kingston, Jamaica, has also grown mainly in this century, but, partly because it was never a tightly defended site, it has

been able to spread without becoming entirely deformed. It is, in colonial terms, an old city. The original British settlement there was at Port Royal, on the spur of land which partly closes the sheltered bay. In June 1692, at a time when (according to a contemporary account) 'the island was full of Gay Hopes, Wallowing in Riches and Abandoned to Wickedness', it was virtually destroyed by an earthquake and a tidal wave. It was after this that the new city, Kingston, was founded, on the opposite shore. It was designed by Sir Christopher Lilly of the Royal Engineers, on the sort of classic grid pattern that, with modifications, had been suggested (but not adopted) for the rebuilding of the city of London after the Great Fire in 1666.

Roughly a hundred years later, what the maps show is basically still his city, easily contained between two creeks. Its centre is a parade ground, a large rectangular square where the two main streets – King Street and Queen Street – intersect, and in the centre of the parade ground is a church. Jetties fringe the shore, there are two forts up the coast to the east, and a new racecourse beyond the town to the north. There, too, is a property marked 'Admiral's Penn'. Another hundred years on, at the turn of the twentieth century, this little town is still entirely recognizable, but it is beginning to spread beyond the creeks, particularly to the east, in a scatter of gentlemen's villas, small speculative developments (Passmore Town, Scotts Town, Franklin Town), a yacht club, a penitentiary, and a lunatic asylum. The racecourse is still in use, but is becoming surrounded by the built-up area, still extending along the lines of the original grid. Mico's College has appeared to the north of it. Further out is a large military camp and a rifle range. Admiral's Penn is now the site of cemeteries. The parade ground in the city centre has lost its church, and has become a formal public garden, with a grandstand; a Public Works Office occupies one corner.

Turn to the map of today and, though the central area is still clearly recognizable, the change in scale is dramatic, The Parade Gardens have become Victoria Park; the racecourse is the King George VI Memorial Park. A stadium has appeared in the region of the military camp, and the rifle range is occupied by a sports complex – but the great

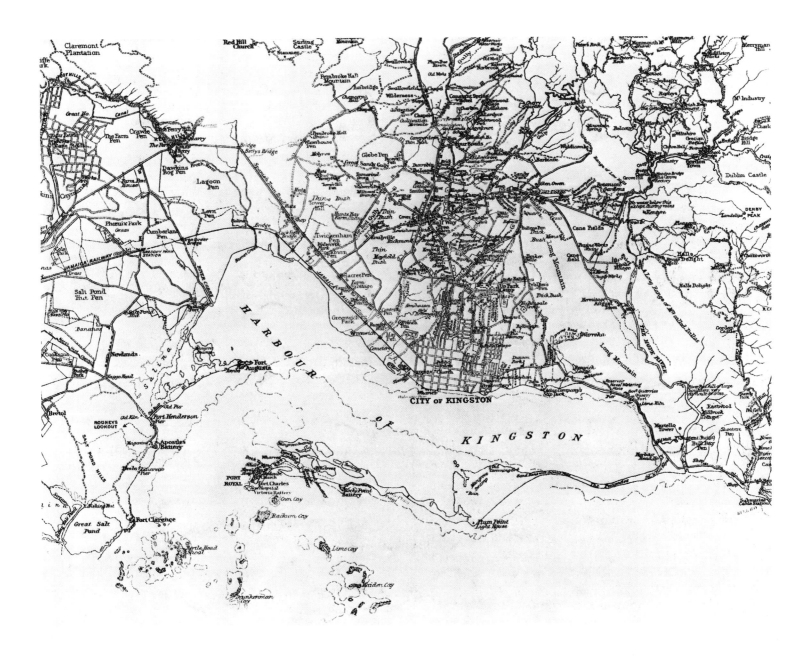

Kingston, Jamaica, c 1910.

difference is in what lies all around and beyond. For Kingston has become a city of close on one million inhabitants, stretching for miles through new suburbs, jumping hills and creeks and continuing onwards, a tidal wave of twentieth-century development.

Happier is the colonial city which achieves success in its early days, and which may thereby hope to achieve a central area which is not quite dwarfed by later transformation. In this respect one of the big success stories must be Melbourne. There never was a penal settlement there: instead, Melbourne seems to have sprung into being as a ready-made English city, looking down on all its rivals. In 1835 it did not exist; there were then only fourteen people counted in the whole of the area that was to become the state of Victoria. By the following year, however, there were two hundred-odd people, free settlers moving from Tasmania; and in 1851 Victoria became a separate colony. In the same year gold was discovered at Ballarat, a hundred miles away from the site of Melbourne, and a rush of people began to land there, in Hobson's Bay. It is said that in one week alone ten thousand people landed, brought by the new steamships which were steadily making transport across the world both quicker and cheaper. It is a measure of the extent to which those locally in power were in control of the situation, however, that the new town did not spring up on the seashore, but a couple of miles inland on the north bank of the River Yarra-Yarra, and in a planned manner. By 1867 Melbourne proper numbered forty-eight thousand in its suburban townships.

A description of the Melbourne of those days comes from a book cheerfully entitled *Victoria: the British el Dorado, or Melbourne in 1869*, by 'A Colonist of twenty years' standing'. 'A Colonist' must, therefore, have known the site in its pre-gold-rush days, and seen it all grow before his eyes:

The city of Melbourne ... is laid out in the form of a rectangular parallelogram, or oblong, divided into eighteen streets crossing each other at right-angles. Its main frontage (its base line, so to speak) is to Flinders Street, on the widest part of the Yarra – the basin where the shipping lies. Flinders Street, with its great, sombre-looking, but business-like warehouses, built of dark blue stone, fronts and overlooks the wharves with their steamers, as well as the railway station with its great goods depot, and the neat and spacious fish-market. At right angles to, and back from, Flinders Street, run nine other streets over hilly ground. They are each more than half a mile in length, and are continued to outside the city. They have a uniform width of ninety-nine feet, are macadamised throughout, and provided with flagged footways twelve feet wide. The centre one of these nine streets is called Elizabeth Street; in point of position it stands the lowest, and seems to run almost on dead level. It is in fact a valley between two adjacent hills, over which extend eight streets, four on each side ... As Elizabeth Street is the centre of the block in its narrowest breadth, so Bourke Street is the main and central street of its greatest length ... During any fine afternoon, Bourke Street is thronged with pedestrians; but in the evening, and especially on Saturday nights, when the lamps and shop fronts are in full blaze of gas-light, one sees, on looking down the street from the Houses of Parliament, an endless concourse of people crowding this great thoroughfare – a spectacle which is enhanced by the glare of lamps which fringe the vista on both sides – and the buzz and hum of many voices. If you want to see a crowd as dense and motley as that of Oxford Street and Tottenham Court Road combined – go to Bourke Street, Melbourne.

But although this enthusiastic citizen praises the 'unusual width of the streets and the palatial appearance of the buildings', and comments on the surprising fact that most of this rapidly constructed town was of stone or brick, not

---

OPPOSITE *The city of Melbourne: a typical gridiron plan allowing unlimited space for expansion.*

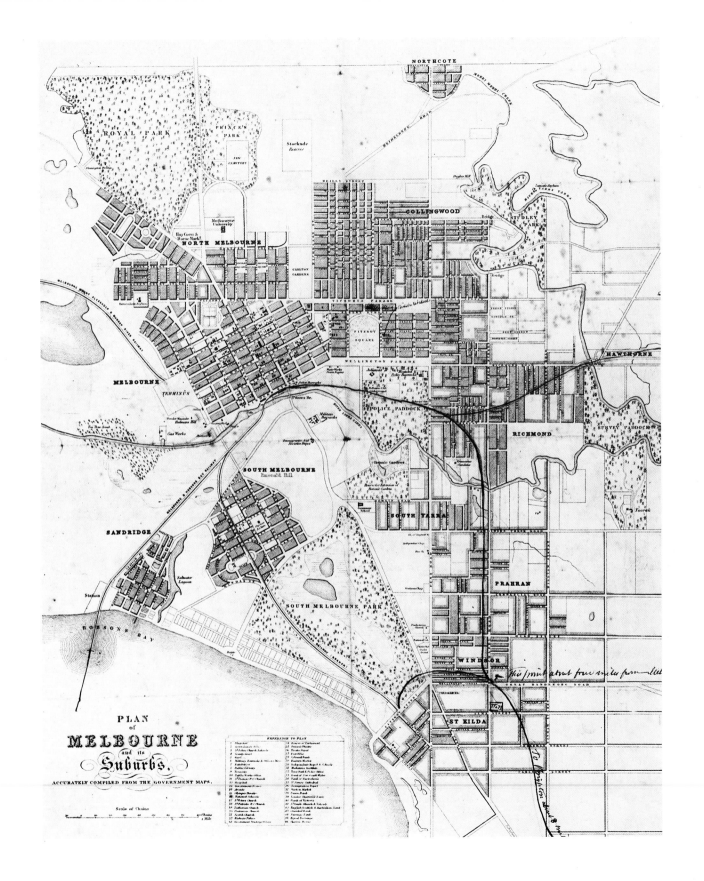

PLAN
of
MELBOURNE
and its
Suburbs.

ACCURATELY COMPILED FROM THE GOVERNMENT MAPS.

Scale of Chains

wood, clearly the problems of erecting a British town in an essentially alien habitat had not yet been fully surmounted. Parks full of subtropical vegetation were all very well (Melbourne is well supplied with these), but –

Elizabeth Street is only twenty-two feet above the level of the sea, and when the rain comes down (as it sometimes does with tropical violence in Melbourne) this street becomes flooded, and acts the part of a great wide open sewer, along which rushes – crossing Flinders Street and falling into the Yarra-Yarra – an immense accumulation of rainwater, mixed with sewage matter.

At the date when this was written, another spacious grid-pattern port city, whose fortunes were also founded partly on gold (Yukon gold), was just being inconspicuously begun on the far side of the Pacific. Although in Canada, its trading orientation was, like that of the Australian ports, towards Asia. It was in about 1870 that Captain 'Gassy' Jack Deighton retired from the sea and opened a saloon beside the lumber wharf and sawmill, which were all that then existed there on a sheltered creek by the delta of the Frazer River, on the north-west coast of the North American continent. For the first twenty years of its life the settlement was modestly called Gastown after its founder, and was built largely of wood, but after 1890, when the Canadian Pacific Railway reached it, the city's future importance looked assured. Settlers began coming in their thousands, including large numbers of Scots and Norwegians – and Chinese from across the ocean. A cycle of world evolution, which had begun in the sixteenth century with Europeans landing on the shores of Asia and America, was completed by Asians continuing the loop of transport round the other side of the globe and meeting there the descendants of Europeans as the indigenous inhabitants. The burgeoning city was given the newer, grander name of 'Vancouver', after the first explorer to chart that coast. A ground plan for 1891 shows the land for miles east of the original port being parcelled out into regular lots, systematically hatched in piece by piece. Grand buildings soon began to go up, including a handsome station and the

Hudson Bay Company building, a five-storey brick warehouse that was then the tallest building in western Canada. The bay and the snow-capped mountains behind it provided a fine setting for a city that, like Melbourne, was essentially a rational creation, an archetypal trading place. Later, the Canadian Railway, too, made Vancouver its terminus. A modern commentator writes: 'The *emptiness* (as well as the extraordinary physical beauty) of most of British Columbia cannot be over-emphasized, with Vancouver a great metropolis on the very edge of the narrow fringe of human habitation' (Donald Olsen, in a personal communication).

Such cities, however successful in their own terms, are less than fascinating historically. Indeed, though both Vancouver and Melbourne are today technically still 'colonial' (or at any rate, Commonwealth cities), one might question whether they have ever been truly 'colonial' at all in the Indian or African sense of the term, and hence in their architecture. It could be argued that, barring Government House in Melbourne, both cities are, rather, examples of another prototype, the New World city, as exemplified all over the United States. In what way does Vancouver differ from Seattle, U.S.A, just down the coast? Hardly at all. Or, come to that, in what essential quality does Melbourne differ from Chicago, another mid-nineteenth-century success story? Or Chicago from Detroit? There is a fundamental distinction to be made between the kind of colonization which imposes an alien culture upon an existing, indigenous one, forming a synthesis with it, and the kind that *takes over* the land and re-creates it as a new place. The distinction is not quite absolute: the colonization of Africa might be regarded as representing a variable mean between these two extremes. But when you reflect that the cities the British planted in India, including their great governmental show-place, are now entirely possessed and run by Indians, whereas those other Indians known to the early New England settlers have left absolutely *no trace* in the lands that were once theirs, except a smattering of place names (Manhattan, Massachusetts, Connecticut), then the gulf of difference between what we mean by 'colonial' in the one context, and what we mean by it in the other, becomes apparent.

Let us return, therefore, to the Indian colonial cities, which started out as defended trading posts in a profoundly alien land, and which, however much they eventually influenced that land, never went near to making it a 'British place' in the sense that Canada or Australia are British places. It was never British society in general that was re-created in India, only selected sections of it. Except for the large force of private soldiers, who were a special category, and in any case lodged in their own barracks, there was never a British working class in India. The nearest thing to it was the Eurasian lower-middle-class community which gradually emerged in the big cities, and on which the railways and many of the offices came to depend – but even these people lived in a style considerably above (and anyway quite different from) that of the ordinary Indian in the street. To be white (or even off-white) was almost invariably to occupy a middle- to upper-class position, and this was as true in the seventeenth century as it was in the twentieth. Thus, when one is talking of the three big original colonial cities of India – Calcutta, Bombay, and Madras – even though one may be talking about cities which appear, visually, to be 'illegitimate children of London and Manchester' in social terms and, therefore, architectural ones, the British contribution is only part of the jigsaw. One is talking about a Manchester with grand Gothic public buildings but no districts of decent brick back-to-backs; a London with parks and palatial town houses, but whose markets and suburbs both derive from another way of life.

At their inception, these cities were not regarded as settling places. In practice, such were the exigencies of life and death in the early days that many of those who came there never went away again. The journey home, round the Cape by sailing ship, took many months and cost the equivalent of thousands of pounds in relative terms, while life for a European frequently turned out, in the Indian climate, to be all too brief. Attitudes to India were essentially predatory rather than empire-building: it was a quick fortune men sought there, not a life's career. And the relatively small number of women to find their way there were often not wives dutifully following their husbands but fortuneless girls staking all – frequently life itself – on making a better match there than they could hope for at home. The Calcutta of those days was evoked, a hundred years or so later, by Kipling, who was sometimes wrong on facts but never on Indian atmosphere, in a description of Park Street Cemetery and a 'big and stately tomb, sacred to "Lucia", who died in 1776 AD aged 23':

What pot-bellied East Indiaman brought the 'virtuous maid' up the river? . . . She was a fair Kentish maiden, sent out, at a cost of five hundred pounds English money, under the Captain's charge, to wed the man of her choice, and *he* knew Clive well, had had dealings with Omichand, and talked to men who had lived through the terrible night in the Black Hole. He was a rich man, Lucia's battered tomb proves it, and he gave Lucia all that her heart could wish . . . And when the convoys came up the river, and the guns thundered, and the servants of the Honourable East India Company drank to the king's health, be sure that Lucia before all the other ladies in the fort had her choice of the new stuffs from England and was cordially hated in consequence . . . She was a toast far up the river. And she walked in the evening on the bastions of Fort William and said 'La! I protest!' It was there that she exchanged congratulations with all her friends on the twentieth of October, when those who were alive gathered together to felicitate themselves on having come through another season; and the men – even the sober factor saw no wrong here – got most royally and Britishly drunk on Madeira that had twice rounded the Cape. But Lucia fell sick, and the doctor – he who went home after seven years with five lakhs and a half, and a corner of the vast graveyard to his account – said that it was a pukka or putrid fever, and the system required strengthening. So they fed Lucia on curries, and mulled wine worked up with spirits and fortified with spices, for nearly a week; at the end of which time she closed her eyes on the weary river and the fort forever . . . (*The City of Dreadful Night*)

The fort is the Fort William we know today, on the Esplanade Maidan, which was cleared as a field of fire – a basic pattern that survives today in all three of the Indian

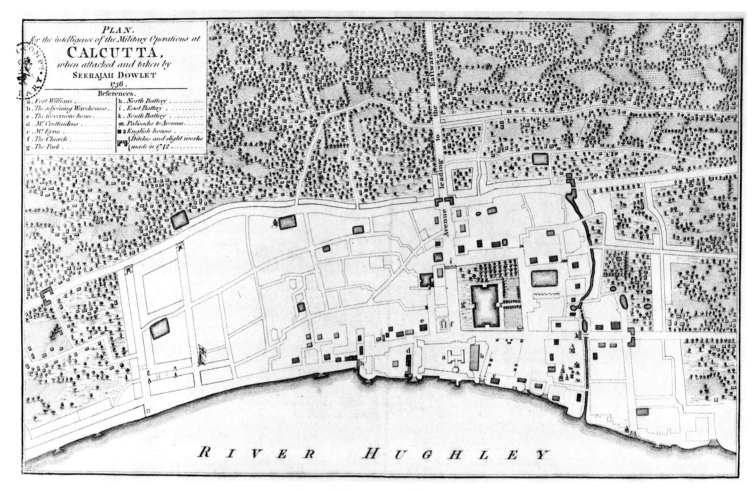

Plan of Calcutta, 1756. Calcutta was
the creation of trading interests.

cities, and also in Cape Town. But the plans for this fort, and indeed the Maidan, date only from 1757 after the Battle of Plassey, and the structure was not complete until 1773, when Lucia came to walk on its bastions. The name derives from King William, of Job Charnock's day, and the original fort lay half a mile up river near the Great Tank (Dalhousie Square). In the early eighteenth century it was the centre of a small, unwalled settlement. It survived into the nineteenth century, when it was used as a custom house. Later the Post Office was built on the site. *Murray's Guide* for 1891 remarks:

The eighty-foot wall of the Post Office is all that remains of the Fort – a row of arches ten foot high in the wall. The place is now used as a workshop, with stables at the west end. According to some authorities, the Black Hole was at the second arch where you enter.

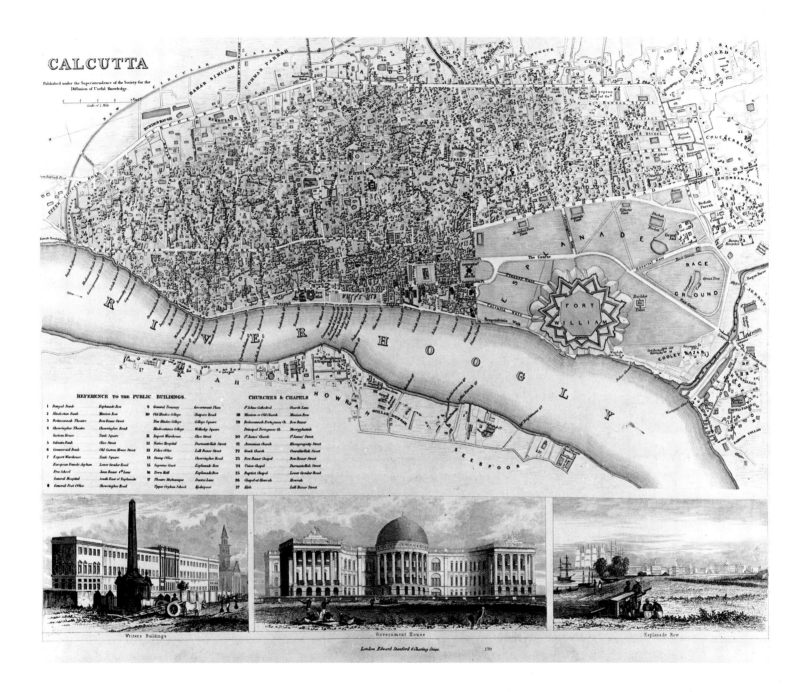

Calcutta in 1856. The effects of commercial success have been dramatic.

93

Most of this disappeared, however, when the Reserve Bank Building was built in 1938. What is particularly striking about the earliest plan of Calcutta is that the Maidan itself, along with Chowringhee and its 'jute-wallah pallaces' (*sic*), does not exist. Instead its site, like all the land surrounding the small settlement, is sprinkled with trees and with what appear to be small native houses. A Governor's House and various prominent merchants' houses are marked within the settlement, but of course Wyatt's grand Government House is not yet there and nor is St John's Church. But on the present site of St John's appears the oldest British graveyard – an inevitable part of any colonial settlement and usually found, as here, right on the edge of the built-up area.

Part of the graveyard still survives today, and with it Job Charnock's mausoleum and several other early and illustrious tombs. In this, Calcutta has been luckier than Bombay, whose oldest cemetery, located near the harbour shore immediately outside the wall of the settlement in the early eighteenth century, was long lost even to record. It was only rediscovered in the twentieth century by a persistent antiquarian who watched men at work on the foundations

for a new Council Hall (near the present-day Jehangir Art Gallery). But Bombay underwent a greater transformation in the late nineteenth century than Calcutta, and the skeleton of the original fortified settlement there is more deeply hidden – though still discernible – than that of Calcutta or Madras.

By the late eighteenth century, Calcutta had, with the new fort and cleared Maidan, taken on essentially the shape it has today. Chowringhee was there, though not yet named, and some large houses were beginning to appear along it. All the development was then still, and for a long time to come, on the east side of the river: there was as yet no bridge. It was also still a much-wooded town: what are marked on contemporary maps as 'bazaars' often look more like houses in coconut groves. The town ended at Circular Road – a piece of British town planning typical of the era: compare the bypass 'New Road' constructed *circa* 1760 on what it was hoped would remain the edge of London (today's Pentonville, Euston, and Marylebone Roads). The new cemetery, Park Street Cemetery where Lucia lies, then marked the south-eastern extent of the town limits. Old cemeteries are

A block of flats on the corner of Octerlony Road, Calcutta.

*Chowringhee Road, looking towards St John's Church,
Calcutta: late nineteenth century.*

like bench marks, reliably indicating how far a town had spread by the date of their oldest graves. Late eighteenth-century Calcutta was roughly contained between the Maratha Ditch and Tolly's Nullah, although there was the beginning of a settlement towards Kiddapore, south of the Maidan, and Warren Hastings' grand house at Alipore, built with marble brought from Benares.

The main difference between Lucia's Calcutta and that which appears on the map of 1825 is that the later town is considerably more Europeanized. The loose network of lanes leading nowhere in particular which characterizes a 'native' town has been replaced over a sizeable area by formal arrangements of streets and squares – the latter often with an oval tank as the centrepiece: College Square,

Wellington Square, Wellesley Square. The basic model is now clearly a Georgian townscape, and grand classical buildings – the Town Hall, the Supreme Court, Government House – have appeared. A racecourse is laid down on the Maidan, with an ornamental serpentine tank in its middle; also an Insane Hospital and a Soldiers' Burial Ground. Across Tolly's Nullah are a jail (the second), various orphan schools, some military lines, and large detached houses beginning to spread along the Garden Reach towards Kiddapore.

One hundred years later, in the early twentieth century, this great alternative London, this metropolis, now darkened – like its mother metropolis – with smoke, and smelling of drains, was still fundamentally the same; it merely spread much further. The racecourse on the Maidan had been joined by a cricket ground, the Victoria Memorial, a number of stern bronze horsemen, and some ornamental gardens. Many, but not all, of the tanks had disappeared from the town squares. More significantly, canals had been built, supplanting the old Ditch and Nullah, feeding into docks both up and down river. Railways, too, had come, converging on the canal outlets and encircling the town. Another line, the Port Trust Railway, had appeared along the river front itself, changing for ever the vista that had greeted generations of travellers upon their arrival. Like Bombay and Madras, like Cape Town (whose railway ended up under the very walls of the ancient castle and nearly succeeded in sweeping it away), Calcutta had to suffer the physically traumatic insertion of railways into an urban pattern which was already well developed – though Calcutta solved part of its problem by establishing its biggest station at Howrah, on the relatively undeveloped western bank of the Hooghly. The other station (Sealdah) was established just east of Circular Road, near the spot where Charnock's banyan tree is supposed to have stood, now an area of quintessential Calcutta squalor. The role of the railway when it came to these old colonial cities was much the same as in London – a disruptive and despoiling force. Very different were its effect and placing in the cities of the New World that were created by the railway, or in Mombasa, which was revived by it.

When writing of Calcutta as the great imperial metropolis, Kipling dismissed Bombay as 'too green, too pretty and too stragglesome', and as for Madras, it 'died long ago'. An exaggeration, of course, but one with a degree of truth in it. In the eighteenth century, Madras (founded very early in 1639) was the most successful and, therefore, the most coherently laid out of the three presidency cities, but later Calcutta and then Bombay overtook it in economic importance and size. As a result, it has today retained much of its period charm, and even some of the look it must have had two hundred years before, while the other two cities have both become victims of their own success, and are monstrously swollen, overcrowded and polluted.

In his book *European Architecture in India: 1750–1850*, Sten Nilsson suggests that Madras was designed on the lines of an ideal European city, on a uniform grid pattern, and contrasts this with the haphazard and 'organic' growth of Indian towns. Europeans did not, however, have the monopoly of regular, centralized street patterns (see Baroda, Jaipur etc.). The essential difference is, surely, not one of culture but of genesis. Settlements that are expected from the first to become towns, and are built up quickly, naturally tend to have a more regular pattern than those which have grown imperceptibly out of villages over the centuries. This is as true of New World ones as it is of colonial ones. In any case the oldest reliable survey of Madras, made *circa* 1702 under the direction of Sir Thomas Pitt, does not suggest a comprehensive, European town plan, Renaissance-style, but rather a tiny, walled, medieval type of settlement, sandwiched between the sea and a bend in the river, with a canal cutting providing a partial moat for it. Its centre is a fort, not yet heavily defended, and with no field of fire. Near at hand are a church, a town hall (with a dome), a Great Pagoda, a burial place unusually situated *within* the walls, and several rows of European-style houses, some of them brick and more than one storey high, with secluded gardens behind them. This is the 'White Town'. Immediately outside the walls to the north and west, the settlement continues in a large suburb of more houses with gardens marked as the 'Black Town': here the houses were apparently mostly clay, thatched and windowless. A large number of the inhabitants were 'Topazes or Portuguese Indians' (of mixed race, that is), and also Armenians. This Black Town peters out into individual formal gardens, the 'Pagans' Burying Place', 'Jews' Burying Place', and the 'Place where the Indians burn their Dead'. Beyond lie swampy plantations. On the other side of the town, where the river forms a great curve, is an island, laid out with 'groves' of trees, 'the Great Walk made by Governor Pitt', the slaughter house, and the powder magazine.

Much of this was swept away later in the century. Some clearance of houses round the fort and further defence work, taking in a detached chunk of island, had been done by

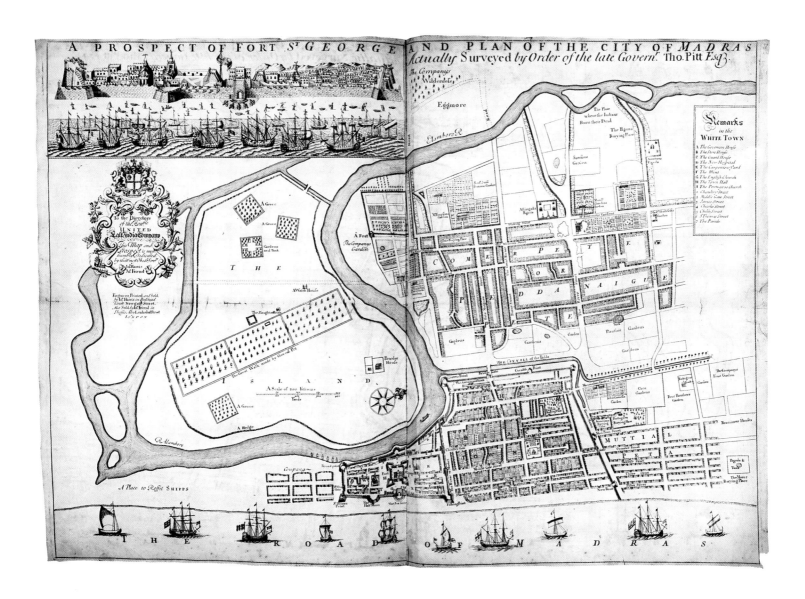

Madras in the mid-eighteenth century.

1746, when the French temporarily captured the place, but after the British got it back again the same transformation as at Calcutta was effected: the old Fort St George was virtually replaced with a new construction on the same site, complete with fortifications in the style of Vauban (Louis XIV's chief military engineer) and almost all the land covered by the original White Town was made into open space, which it remains today. Effectively, the old suburb had now become the town, extended and furnished with town walls. By the end of the century the swampy plantation areas were also being colonized with detached houses, and Madras was acquiring the splendid fringe of classical buildings along the beach – Bentinck's Building, the Custom House, and so on – which are still there.

In the course of the next seventy years, gardens and more detached houses came, but Madras was not transformed in character by the pressures of urbanization. The enormous increase in world trade polarized itself, in India, on the two big ports, and Madras, less well placed, could not compete – though a harbour was constructed in front of the beach in the 1860s. (The whole of that south-east coast, from Ceylon to Orissa, has no natural harbour.) In the same decade, the town walls, which had survived more or less intact, were replaced by railway lines. By this time the Chepauk Palace and its gardens across the river to the south, the old seat of the Nawabs of the Carnatic, had been acquired by the British Government, and along this shore a new run of public buildings began to go up, replacing the original ones in terms of prestige. In the stately words of *Murray's Guide* for 1891:

The Marina, the fashionable drive and promenade at Madras, is by the sea-shore, from the southern extremity of the Fort southward over the Napier Bridge, and past the Senate House, the Revenue Board Office, the Civil Engineering College, the Department of Public Works Offices, the Presidency College, as far as the Capper House Hotel. Then Cathedral Road runs nearly due W. about two miles to St George's Cathedral, the Mount Road, and the suburb of Adyar. A great part of these roads is overhung by mighty banian [*sic*] trees, forming a tunnel through which one drives in agreeable coolness even when the sun is hot.

Not so much a dead city, one would say, as a sleeping one.

A nineteenth-century view of the Madras foreshore.

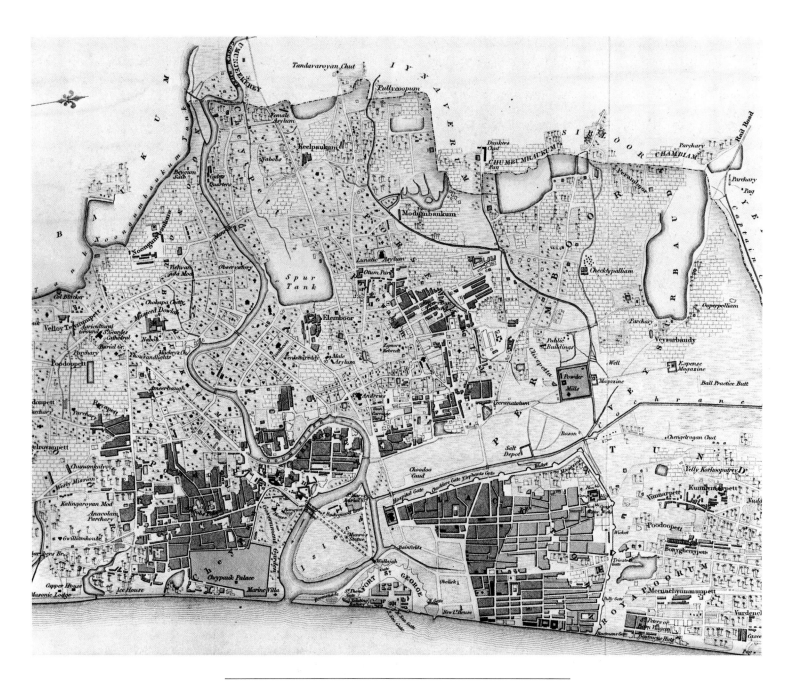

Madras, early nineteenth century. With the threat of war over,
the city had developed extensive and attractive garden suburbs.

Comparable improvements were made over the same period of time in Bombay, but with the difference that, in Bombay, the demolition of old walls and the construction of new public buildings were simply one aspect of a great paroxysm of growth and change that gripped the city from the 1860s onwards. What was (and is) known as the Fort in Bombay was, confusingly, never a fort but a castle within a small, walled settlement not dissimilar from the original construction at Madras. It was this entire, compact settlement – about a mile in length and half a mile wide, and occupied by both natives and Europeans – that was given progressively stronger defences as the eighteenth century went on. Around the mid-century, when the French were causing alarm in Bombay by attacking the towns on the far side of India, all the huts and plantations for a thousand feet beyond these walls were cleared away, and this field of fire is still visible as Bombay's chain of maidans. It was on the far side of this open space that the Black Town gradually developed, and the difference in character between this bazaar area and the downtown big business and municipal section of the city persists clearly to this day. No fortifications can now be found, however: the old castle on the shore is inaccessibly buried in the naval dockyard, and the walls, being town walls, went with the mid-nineteenth century improvements.

It seems worthwhile making the point here that one should not trust the parochial explanations, commonly provided by local history, for urban change. Books on Bombay will tell you that the Fort walls were pulled down, and a boulevard with grand new buildings laid out in their place, because of the remarkable economic boom enjoyed by Bombay in the early 1860s, when cotton supplies from America to England were cut off as a consequence of the Civil War and the price of cotton exported from Bombay rose greatly in consequence. But the fact of the matter is that the walls of Old Bombay were pulled down in exactly the same year as those of Old Vienna (for which event, of course, quite other reasons are adduced); and, indeed, at this time walls were falling – and railways coming in, and docks and factories being built – all over Europe. What we see

happening in Bombay in the 1860s and 1870s, and also to some extent in Calcutta and Madras, is simply a concrete example of the global forces of the period and of Britain's unique world position of industrial power. The wealth her Empire brought her wrought great changes in her own cities; and these changes were, in their turn, exported back to India. What was being enacted in booming Bombay in the last three decades of the century is essentially what was also being enacted in London, Manchester, Leeds, Birmingham, Bradford and Sheffield.

In Bombay, as in Calcutta, the settlement's original relationship with the sea – which was its *raison d'être* – has been very much altered and disrupted over the course of time. In Calcutta, the Hooghly is silting up; shipping is declining, and, as I have said, the railway has cut off the city from its shore. Bombay remains a major world port – indeed, it currently does more refitting of ships than any other – but its original sheltered harbour has been totally swallowed by the docks that run right up the eastern edge of the island. Back Bay, on the western side, where the new, fine array of governmental buildings was constructed after 1860, was similarly despoiled by a railway line along its strand in the closing years of the nineteenth century, but such is the endemic nature of land reclamation works in Bombay that in the twentieth century a whole new shoreline has been constructed beyond the railway, complete with a yet newer set of prestigious buildings. Bombay is, indeed, the most factitious of cities, its present land-mass having only a very sketchy affinity with what was there when the founders came. Similarly, in Cape Town, the nucleus of the town – already confined by geographical contours – was hedged in on its open, seaward side in the late nineteenth century by the laying of a railway along the strand, and since then this barrier has been thickened by the addition of a road on the reclaimed foreshore.

The early maps of Cape Town bear a marked resemblance to those of Madras, in that the town then consisted of a Vauban fort on the shore, the Castle, with an adjacent open space – the Parade Ground – and, beyond, a compact, grid-pattern town in the lee of the Lion's Head hill. In the

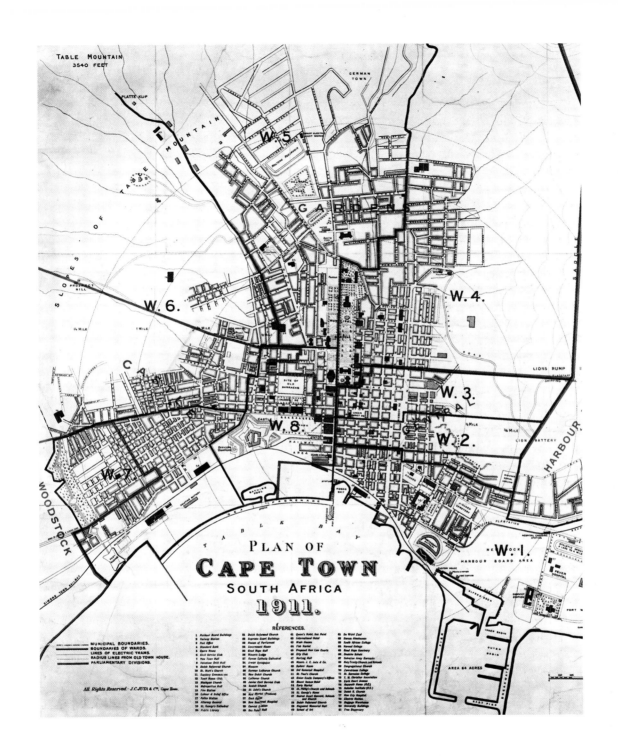

Cape Town in 1911.

nineteenth century, it was below this flagstaff hill, further round the shore, that the usual appurtenances of every colonial station gradually ranged themselves – the wharfs, the battery, the docks, the hospital, the lighthouse, the prestigious new church, the racecourse, the winding road of detached villas with a view of the bay. Today, as in Kingston, Jamaica, the racecourse has become a public garden, and the low-rise, Dutch-Colonial buildings are being replaced by high blocks, but the essential shape and character of the place has not changed. It is unusual in that at the heart of this city lies a large botanical garden, which was first laid out by Jan van Riebeeck of the Dutch East India Company in 1652. None other of the original, indespensible Company gardens of that era has survived.

I have said that no colonial town can be seen today in its original form. But different parts of the world seem to be running on different clocks: some of the towns I have mentioned were new settlements when others were already in, or past, their prime. Much of Africa was only just being explored when India was already mapped and parcelled out, and some of the African colonial cities in the twentieth century recall, therefore, in a somewhat hallucinatory manner, counterparts elsewhere at an earlier date. Freetown, Sierra Leone, for instance, though founded by freed slaves at the end of the eighteenth century under the auspices of Wilberforce, has remained tiny. In an echo of Cape Town, the whole of the centre is occupied by a large hill, the site of the fort and erstwhile Government House. The waterfront has a jail, a hospital, some jetties, a modest cathedral, and an even smaller custom house. Writing in the 1950s, when the place was still a British crown colony, Elspeth Huxley said:

Behind the silk cotton trees rises the solid Victorian façade of the law-courts, embellished with heavy, curved, rococo sculpture; most of the buildings are heavy, too, and dark red, the red of dried blood; the bay below is azure, speckled with white sails.

Except for the colour of the buildings, it might be an early nineteenth-century port that is thus described.

But the quintessential time-travelling experience is provided in Mombasa, situated on a small island on the edge of Kenya (formerly British East Africa). It lies up the coast from Zanzibar, and for a long time was leased by the Sultan of Zanzibar to the British. There was a city here a thousand years ago, and in the seventeenth century the Portuguese built one of their forts here, but when a traveller visited it in 1883 he recorded that,

Except the fort and some walls, there is little left to tell of Portuguese occupation. Everywhere ruins of houses and mosques tell the tale of decayed grandeur, of the loss of former spirit, energy, and enterprise.' (H. P. Thompson)

A decade later, the railway had come; and in the early twentieth century a new colonial city of low-rise white houses, roofed with Mangalore tiles from across the Arabian Sea, rose on the foundations of the old Arab dwellings. The creek separating the island from Africa proper was dredged; and there is a deep-water port there next to the railway depot, and an oil refinery, though there is still a small *dhow* harbour in the lee of the fort. The vista from the sea is of waves breaking on a rocky shore, palm trees, and a row of sparkling public buildings just as in Old Madras – the lighthouse, the judge's house, Government House, the Police Commissioner's house, the hospital, the military headquarters, and finally Fort Jesus with the public gardens and the law courts just behind it. On the other side of the fort is the Mombasa Club, said even today to be a haven of British-style tranquillity and cucumber sandwiches.

The town, universally liked by visitors, also has a particularly good red light district. That, too, has always been an essential ingredient of the archetypal colonial city.

*The botanical gardens, Cape Town, which were laid out
in 1652. The dome in the background belongs to
the university building designed by Hawke and McKinlay.*

Public Buildings

Colin Amery

IT IS A CURIOUS FACT that the largest empire that the world has ever known left behind not a series of architectural triumphs but a remarkably mixed bag of public buildings. Like the character of the British people themselves, the style is elusive, often reticent, and only occasionally rampant and splendid. The monarchy, with its gloved, garden-party manners, has left a more permanent impression than the buildings erected for the performance of public rituals.

Democracy and the rule of law do not necessarily produce great aesthetic or architectural achievements, whereas autocratic aggrandisement somehow produces the finest concrete statements of faith. When the Earl of Rosebery spoke in Adelaide, Australia, in the winter of 1884, about the Empire's being a commonwealth of nations, he had defined its very nature. Even at its height, it was more of a loose association of countries that reflected its piecemeal origins than a tightly-knit band of like-minded nations intent on its own development. The Government of the Empire did not depend upon grandiose new cities and elaborate centres of government. It was the crown alone that kept things together; and its representatives, the Viceroys, the Governor-Generals, the Governors, Residents, Administrators and High Commissioners, lived in their outposts as though they were back home on their estates. Even the grandest of all the imperial public buildings – the Viceroy's house in Calcutta – was merely a reproduction of a grand English country house, with the whole subcontinent as its estate.

Because the earliest British settlements depended upon trade with the Americas and the Indies, no certainty existed that there would be a need for more than a network of trading stations, no one having at that time a clear idea of how long the British would remain. The kind of architecture required for a buccaneering base is very different from that required for an elaborate system of colonial administration. Thus in the earliest days, towards the end of the 1500s, settlers built domestic rather than governmental quarters – a meeting house or a church is often the first public indication of the British presence in the West Indies, those Carribean islands which were the first English colonies. St Kitts was settled in 1623, Barbados in 1627, Nevis in 1629, Antigua and Monserrat in 1632 – and the Bahamas have enjoyed British rule since 1666. Somehow, these islands, with their sugar crop and future slave trade, have a heady and potent atmosphere of piracy and indolence. It is beguiling, and has, perforce, had its effect on the architecture. The great King's House in Spanish Town, Jamaica, was built for the British Governor by the chief engineer, Craskell, who was not a trained architect. Typical of its date, 1762, there is something of a colonial timelag in its design: it is more like an early eighteenth-century country house in England, with its gigantic portico shading the long, plain façade. This is a true example of the architecture emerging in the West Indies by the 1740s, and in the more southerly colonial settlements on the mainland of North America.

It is in Spanish Town, Jamaica, that we can see what is probably the finest group of British colonial buildings in the

West Indies. King's Square has the grand façade of the King's House on the west, with the Rodney Memorial on the north. On the eastern side of the square is the former House of Assembly, with the grand Courts of Justice to the south. This was the Jamaican capital until 1872, and it is a microcosm of colonial rule. It too was designed by Craskell, about whom virtually nothing is known, and it links together the principal qualities of British colonial rule. The Governor represents the monarch in a house that, as nearly as possible, is a replica of a Palladian pile in England. The Parliament represents the early growth of democracy under the rule of law, dispensed by gowned and bewigged judges under the fans of the panelled courtrooms in the West Indian heat. The fourth side of this imperial piazza explains how it originated. The Rodney Memorial was built in 1785 to commemorate Admiral Rodney's victory over the French in the Battle of the Saints in 1782. It takes the form of an octagonal dome and cupola over a highly romanticized statue of the hero by the sculptor John Bacon. This shrine to British naval and military success is linked to the adjacent buildings by an Ionic colonnade and a parapet at first-floor level.

In architectural terms it is a town, like Falmouth in Jamaica, that accurately captures the flavour of the kind of life that was lived in the settlement. It was an agreeable one for the plantation owners and the civil servants who

*The Rodney Memorial in Spanish Town,
Jamaica, built in 1785.*

The House of Assembly, Spanish Town, Jamaica, built in 1762.
It now houses the Parish Council Offices.

accompanied the growth of the Empire. Falmouth has the atmosphere of an English town such as Weymouth or Sidmouth – streets of eighteenth- and early nineteenth-century houses of stone, brick and clapboard, with delicately curved, wrought-iron balconies and roofs which originally had cedar shingles. Here in the domestic realm the particularly Jamaican feature of a 'cooler' was developed, fixed or moveable louvres alternating with the glazed sashes to provide shade. The Court House at Falmouth is one of the best public buildings. It was erected in 1817 –

totally Classical in design, with a grand portico over a double stairway that leads to the main rooms on the first floor. It was built of the local white stone, and then whitewashed. The high Palladian style exactly suits the climate and light of the West Indies, and the palms and yuccas that surround the Court House give just a hint of the exotic.

On the other islands of the West Indies the diversity of the architecture reflects the muddled history of the area, with many islands frequently changing hands. From the peace

106

The Court House, Falmouth, Jamaica, built c 1817. The building has suffered from poor restoration after a fire in 1926.

treaty of Aix-la-Chapelle in 1748 until the coming of Free Trade in the mid-nineteenth century, there was a period of prosperity and building. No major works of architecture can be recorded, but in the public field colonial classicism was the principal style. New government offices and law courts designed by Nicolson and Carlette were built as late as the 1930s in Kingston, by then the capital of Jamaica.

In Barbados, the Governor's residence, rather unaccountably called Holborn, is the principal public building, though it is of no particular architectural distinction. On the island of Trinidad the official architecture looks more towards South America and the influence of Spain.

Napoleon's plans to colonize as much of the West Indies as he could led to the near encounter of Lord Nelson with Admiral Villeneuve. Nelson would have known the St James's barracks in Port of Spain – solid, serious, early eighteenth-century buildings erected between 1724 and 1727. It is possible even now to imagine Woodford Square, Port of Spain, in its heyday, when at least six different types of colonial architecture surrounded it.

At the Treaty of Paris, which ended the great Seven Years' War between France and England in 1763, Grenada was one of the islands retained by the British. Its capital, St George's, has a series of modest but typical early nineteenth-century public buildings, including a Treasury, a Post Office and the Government House (1802–7). In Nassau, capital of the Bahamas, the buildings are of the same late eighteenth-century to early nineteenth-century Classical type. There is more than a trace of the colonial Georgian style that had become the official architecture of the freed American colonies, a curious adaptation of the style of the conqueror to the American 'Colonial' that so clearly today proclaims Freedom, Democracy and a glorious Republicanism. Williamsburg inspired parts of Nassau: porticoed, stuccoed Georgian – one colony inspiring another. Government House (1803–6), the earlier Post Office, and the government offices (1785), are agreeable, simple, 'timelag' Classical. The Central Library in Nassau, a charming octagon, was originally built by engineers as a prison.

In Trinidad there was much official rebuilding after the great hurricane of 1813. The new Governor, Sir Ralph Woodford, rebuilt the Fire Brigade Headquarters and the Ministerial Building. Later, the Governor-General's House was built to designs by Fergusson between 1873 and 1875, and the General Hospital was built with bricks exported from England. After the Emancipation of the Slaves Act of 1833, the West Indies did not build any more substantial public buildings, despite the fact that the planters were compensated by a grant from Parliament of £20,000,000 – then a fantastic sum.

The thirteen British colonies in North America outside Canada were governed under the old Colonial System. This meant that each colony stood by itself, each having its own Governor appointed by the crown, and its own Legislative Assembly which passed local acts and voted on the sum of the Governor's salary. The New England colonies enjoyed a population of hardy farmers, and a Presbyterian strain in the population ensured high standards of education, maintained at the fine colleges of Yale and Harvard. Virginia developed from its early settlement in 1607 into a land of great estates cultivated by slave labour. In the early seventeenth century, houses and churches, as well as the few government buildings in Massachusetts and New England were all timber-framed and boarded, with classical detail (very occasionally Gothic) made up by carpenters. Glass was imported from England and a typical early building, for example the House of the Seven Gables (*circa* 1635), was a simple timber version of the English model

In Connecticut there were 126,000 colonists by 1756, all of them creating a steady demand for new buildings. Stylistically all early American buildings are plain and decent – amply in tune with the Puritan consciences of the early settlers. New Haven provided a base for the new classicism which was reflected as much in the town planning as in the architecture. The central town square led naturally to the grid. Was it because timber was the principal material that there is a poverty of invention in the public buildings of New England and Connecticut? The churches and the meeting houses are the principal monuments of these colonies.

Williamsburg, in Virginia, was the capital of the colony from 1699 to 1780. The plantation economy, helped by the existence of slaves, was a prosperous one. The re-creation and restoration of the city (from 1926 with the resources of John D. Rockefeller Jr) has given us a very clear and pretty accurate idea of an eighteenth-century American colony. Extending for a mile between the Governor's Palace and the Capitol and the College of William and Mary, Williamsburg is a town of brick and tile public buildings and clapboard houses.

It was the remarkable Colonel Spotswood who designed and laid out the Governor's House. It was later to be ironically christened the Palace because of the immense cost of its construction. It is very much in the Queen Anne style: five bays wide with a steeply pitched roof with five dormers. The central cupola is of double height and towers way above the tall chimneys. The house is formal and the approach grand – along an avenue of catalpa trees where parades and displays of fireworks were held.

The Capitol at Williamsburg was one of the principal

The Governor's Palace, Williamsburg, Virginia. Completed in 1720,
it was destroyed by fire in 1781.
The present building is a reconstruction.

The Capitol, Williamsburg. Originally completed in 1705, the building was reconstructed after being devastated by fire. The House of Burgesses, America's oldest representative assembly, resided here.

buildings of colonial America. It was rebuilt many times but the version that we see today is a reconstruction of the first, built between 1701 and 1705. Steeply pitched roofs are topped by another tall, glazed wooden tower, with a gallery and a flagpole for the Union Flag. Two curved wings are lit on the ground floor by *oeil-de-boeuf* windows.

The College of William and Mary was founded by royal charter in 1693. It is the oldest college in the country after Harvard, and was established to bring to the American colonies the kind of education that was provided in England by Oxford and Cambridge. It had in its charter the added responsibility of 'the conversion of the Indian heathen'. The building was designed in 1694, reputedly by Sir Christopher Wren, but there is little evidence to support this theory. (To ensure accuracy a 'Wren' building is always described as 'being adapted to the nature of the country by the

Gentlemen there'.) Like all the Williamsburg public edifices, it has a high roof and a small central clock tower; the deep, arcaded cloister and the Great Hall of the college are reminiscent of Chelsea Hospital. There is a mixture of small-scale grandeur and folksiness about Williamsburg that is absent from the colonial public buildings of a later date.

After the Declaration of Independence in 1776, the architectural influence was still largely British. The White House, in Washington, was designed in the 1790s by an Irish architect, James Hoban, and the Capitol by the British architect William Thornton, who died in 1818. In Philadelphia the Hall of Independence, although much restored, has good red brickwork, and that mixture of the Classical façade and the spire or tower which was the direct influence of Gibbs' architecture on the designers and craftsmen of North

The Brick Market, Newport, Rhode Island, designed and built by Peter Harrison in 1762.
The ground-floor arches were filled in with windows when the building
was converted into a town hall in the nineteenth century.

*Redwood Library, Newport, Rhode Island. Designed by Peter Harrison
and built in 1748, this is the oldest library
in continuous use in the United States.*

America, dependent on the circulation of copies of his *Book of Architecture* of 1728.

America shows that there is a colonial architecture emerging for public consumption. It remains colonial because it is usually a primitive version of what is going on at home. New England has a feeling of a toy-like imitation of eighteenth-century England.

Moving to the north, the public architecture of Canada immediately appears to have a more broadly based European traditional root. Before the British conquest Canada was part of 'New France', and has to be seen as one of the long line of French colonies from Florida to Nova Scotia. North of New France lay the territories leased to the English Hudson Bay Company – an area that contributed nothing at all to the development of an architectural tradition.

On the eve of the British conquest of Canada's French occupants in 1760 the architectural position was very clearly explained in geographical terms. West and north of the Allegheny Mountains the architectural tradition was completely French; to the south and east of those same mountains the traditions were English. The architecture that concerns us in this book is that of the buildings erected by the British after 1760, and these seem to fall into two types; those buildings that develop the Gothic style and are thus linked into the whole European tradition, and those which continue the more purely English method of building – amateur Classicism.

Later buildings in Canada, in the early years of the twentieth century, are sometimes more influenced by the architectural developments taking place in the United States than by either England or France. Quebec and Montreal both have buildings that date from the seventeenth and early eighteenth centuries that show distinctly how regulated colonial life and its buildings were – with direct instructions from Paris. Not until 1841 were Upper and Lower Canada united to form a single colony. Parliament was to be based at Ottawa – at that time a small village, selected, it is rumoured, by the wandering of Queen Victoria's hatpin over a pink-tinged map of her dominions.

In architectural terms Ottawa is some kind of synthesis that represents the romance of Empire and the sense of the establishment of divinely inspired democracy. The Gothic form of the federal Parliament gives Canada a shrine, a palace of law that adopts the forms of the great cathedrals and colleges of Europe.

It is true to say that in Canada the Gothic carries with it the same sense of historical importance as the Classical Revival does in the United States of America. In the same way that the Classical in America is associated with the birth in 1800 of the new republic, Gothic is to Canada the hallmark of the birth in the 1850s of the new dominion. In both cases the particular style came to be seen as the new nation's first architectural expression. Tracing the Gothic in Canada is the most fruitful approach to her architectural history.

It was in 1811 that the Governor, Sir James Craig, appointed a new commission to organize the planning of new legislature for Quebec. Many Canadians sent in designs, including a remarkable one from François Faillange in a florid, Baroque style. The most interesting ones, however, came from England.

The design signed by Jeffry Wyatville, who was also the architect of Fonthill Abbey, and was later to undertake with such success the restoration of Windsor Castle, hedged its bets. The plan allowed for two alternative elevations – one Classical, of the Ionic Order; the other Gothic, with Perpendicular qualities. Joseph Gandy (1771–1843) also sent a set of plans from England. In the end nothing was built.

In the Maritimes a certain amount of 'Carpenter's Gothic' was to be seen in the domestic field between 1812 and 1840, but French Canada was too preoccupied with the evolution of its own particular blend of Baroque and Classical to pay much attention to the growth of Gothic in the public realm. The best serious Gothic architecture in Canada is to be found in its churches. Christ Church Cathedral in Fredericton, New Brunswick, which was designed by Frank Wills, who came to Canada from Exeter in Devon, is close to the true spirit of Gothic. Wills' knowledge of archaeology gives his ecclesiastical buildings a quality missing from Canada's Gothic public buildings. In Toronto the old building of Trinity College (1851), which adapted the English collegiate models to Canada, is by the Irish architect Kivas Tully (1820–1905). It has all the Tudor qualities of an Oxford college, but the elongation of its turrets and pinnacles gives it an unlikely Islamic appearance. It is interesting to note that the Governor of Canada in 1856 was Sir Edmund Head Bt, who considered himself an authority on art. He took a great interest in the growth of public buildings, and expressed a dislike for the Gothic emphasis of the designs for the University of Toronto by F.W. Cumberland (an architect who had been associated in London with Barry), and recommended as a model the Palazzo Pubblico in Siena. During Sir Edmund's absences from Toronto, the architect concocted a more Romanesque style for the University, with some fine Norman and Romanesque detail that predates Henry Hobson Richardson's revival and development of the Romanesque in Boston, Massachusetts, by about twenty years.

There can be no doubt that the outstanding achievement of the Gothic Revival in Canada is the Canadian Parliament building in Ottawa. It is one of *the* imperial buildings of the British Empire, carrying in its design so much of the Gothic and northerly qualities of the British colonists. It is wonderfully sited on a cliff above the Ottawa River. The architect of the principal building was Thomas Fuller, who

Provincial Government Building, Victoria, British Columbia, built in 1898. Crowning the central dome of the main building is a statue of Captain George Vancouver.

Parliament Buildings, Ottawa, designed by Thomas Fuller
and Chilion Jones and built 1859–65.

was born in Bath, Somerset, in 1822, and who was to become Canada's leading architect.

The Parliament was very much influenced by Ruskin. An early drawing of the river front shows the clear influence of Dean and Woodward's Oxford Museum. Both designs had a strong element of Venetian colouring in the stonework,

both had chapter houses. Fuller supplemented his passion for Ruskin's work by importing towers from Germany and roofs from France; and the long rows of very pointed windows were straight from the Cloth Hall at Ypres. The Parliament was burned down in 1916, except for the library, and rebuilt by the architects Pearson and Marchand in a far grander way, with yet more towers, one added in 1927 as a Tower of Peace to mark the end of the Great War. Ottawa is the shadow of Westminster cast over the icy wastes of Britain's northernmost reaches of Empire. A strangely evocative building that says more in its silhouette about the dreams and aspirations of the imperial ministers than any speech or book about ideals of dominion status.

This great building of confederate Canada overwhelms in architectural terms much of the rest of Canada's public architecture. Frank W. Simon's new Parliament building in Winnipeg, and the Province Building in Halifax, Nova Scotia, are both examples of dull routine official Classicism. John Merrick's work in the early nineteenth century in the Maritimes lacks the lightness of touch of the American Classical architects.

In Toronto the mixture of public buildings exemplifies the stylistic dilemma. Ontario's Houses of Parliament (1885–91) are neo-Grecian and solidly built of Canadian brownstone and granite, Osgoode Hall (1828) is in the plain and elegant High Court style, while the City Hall is grandly Romanesque (1891–1899) with a three-hundred-foot clock-tower. In the 1930s, by which time Canada was completely independent of Britain, Ottawa continued to grow, with new Supreme Court buildings in 1939. The arch and pedestal of the National War Memorial, and the Classical Royal Canadian Mint, are unadventurous. In Quebec, after the Château Normandie of 1805, the most significant public buildings are the extravagant French Renaissance Parliament buildings erected between 1878 and 1892. This is a giant château, more than three hundred feet long with a four-storey central tower and two parliamentary chambers. Nova Scotia was the first overseas colony to achieve full self-government; and Halifax, dominated by Citadel Hill, shows, in the early nineteenth-century Government House and Province Building, signs of the New England influence. Lumber was one of the chief reasons for the exploitation of Canada, and also for the architectural prominence of British Columbian wood.

Until the turn of the century, architecture on the west coast was distinctive because it was more vernacular in style, more closely related to the native materials. The only public building of any consequence is the Provincial Government Building in Victoria, British Columbia. It is in a bizarre and heterogeneous collection of styles by the architect F.W. Rattenbury – Romanesque, Classical and Gothic, with a large granite dome. It is fair to say that the battle of the styles being fought in England reached Canada some fifty years later, and the result is that her colonial public buildings – apart from the romantic Gothic fantasy at Ottawa – lack the conviction and freedom of expression inherent in the much less inhibited nineteenth-century architecture of her neighbour, the United States of America.

The subcontinent of India, however, is more than accustomed to empire builders. It represented to the British an opportunity to fulfil all the aspects of imperial ambition, from trade through to government and control, in the greatest display of imperialism to be seen anywhere in the Empire. India somehow brought out qualities in the British unexpressed anywhere in Africa, or even in the white dominions.

Whether or not it was the presence of preceding imperial regimes that inspired imitation, and indeed rivalry, India was certainly the theatre *par excellence* for a cast of administrators who genuinely felt that they had a mission to bring good government to India and to rule her for ever.

There was a greater opportunity in India than elsewhere for the flowering of the individual ruler: from Wellesley to Curzon the Viceroyalty flourished in a variety of different guises. In turn these men had more than a little influence on the buildings erected for the government of this great country.

Madras, the site of the earliest settlement of the East India Company, dates back to the end of 1639, when the territory was donated by the last representative of the Vijayanagar royal family, and Government House, Madras, set the tone for all the other Governors' residences in India. It was a 'garden house' of the eighteenth century, built originally by a rich Portuguese merchant and standing in seventy-five acres of grounds. The house still stands in a busy quarter of Triplicane, but it turns its back on the town to face the sea across lawns and a lotus-strewn lake. Successive Governors altered and enlarged the original house, but it was not until the arrival of Lord Clive, son of the great Clive of India, that substantial changes were made. He employed John Goldingham, a surveyor and astronomer who lived in Madras, as his architect, who doubled the house in size, adorned it with delicate plasterwork, and erected in the grounds a splendid detached banqueting hall in the style of a Doric temple. It was christened in October, 1802, with a glittering ball to celebrate the Peace of Amiens. The scale of gubernatorial life can be gauged from the fact that there was stabling at the residence for two hundred horses. The house, well suited to the climate of southern India, is surrounded by an immense, two-storey verandah, between whose white pillars were cane *attics*, or sun blinds, damped by servants to keep the rooms cool.

The remainder of Madras's public buildings date from the 1860s and later, and are much influenced by the architect Robert Fellowes Chisholm (1840–1915), who, although essentially a Gothicist, was one of the pioneers in the adoption of native styles in India. His Board of Revenue Offices, formerly Chapauk Palace, is a grand building in the Hindu-Saracenic style of the 1870s with arcades and minarets. Chisholm's Post Office in Madras is not, however, in the native style, but is a curious mixture of Rhenish towers, Gothic arcades, and an unusual roof pierced by

Osgoode Hall, Toronto. Built by the Law Society of Upper Canada in 1829–32, the building is now occupied by the Supreme Court of Canada.

Senate House, University of Madras, designed by Robert Fellowes Chisholm
and built in the 1870s. Chisholm was one of the most
accomplished architects in India in his day.

pointed dormers. He also designed the Senate House of the University, between 1874 and 1879, and the Government presidency college. He frequently used the students of the Madras School of Art, of which he was principal, to execute 'industrial art work'. The largest and most noticeable Indo-Saracenic public building in Madras is the Law Courts, built between 1888 and 1892 to the designs of J.W Brassington and Henry Irwin, assisted by J.H. Stephen. It is a flamboyantly romantic building, which rises to a hundred and sixty feet, and is also used as a lighthouse, the light being visible some twenty miles out to sea. Like so many of the apparently uncoordinated buildings in India, this one is very logically planned. There are separate circulation systems and several open verandahs to keep the rooms cool. In both mass and detail the Law Courts are Gothic Revival, but the cusped arches are Moorish in style. The Victoria

Memorial Hall by Irwin was opened in 1909 – a sophisticated and elegant essay in the Indo-Saracenic style. The Moore Market, the Victoria Public Hall (1883–8), and the Ripon Building (now the Corporation of Madras), the latter with a tower almost a hundred and fifty feet high, are all examples of the late flowering of the Public Works Department.

Madras ceased to be so important to the Empire by the middle of the nineteenth century, Calcutta and Bombay having superseded it. Bombay was considered an unhealthy spot, for its seven islands were, at low tide, surrounded by malarial mud flats. Travellers in the seventeenth century speak of Bombay as a 'charnel house'. And a later visitor, Aldous Huxley, was to write that he considered Bombay to be one of the most appalling cities of either hemisphere, as it had the misfortune to develop during the darkest period of

Middlesex County Court House, London, Ontario.
It was built in 1831.

*Moore Market, Madras: a stylish Indo-Saracenic design
by R. E. Ellis, in red brick with decorative finials.*

Ripon Building, Madras, 1905, housing the city council.
Lord Ripon, in knee breeches, still looks on from the gardens.

ABOVE *Madras Railway Station. In India, as in England,
the British saw railways as a symbol of power and
the modern world, and built their stations accordingly.*

architectural history. Although today Bombay is admired as one of the most complete Victorian Gothic Revival cities to survive anywhere in the world, its architectural reputation has not always stood so high. The British Governors after 1719 retreated from the humid and claustrophobic Government House in the Fort to the Classical splendours of their country house at Parell, which they much preferred. From 1829–85, Parell, which had once been a monastery, became the chief residence of the British Governors of Bombay. It was abandoned after Lady Fergusson, the Governor's wife, died of cholera. From the 1880s British Governors occupied a clutch of comfortable bungalows called Malabar Point, facing the healthy sea-breezes.

Parell was situated on the Island of Bombay, six miles to the north of the city. It was approached from its principal gate by a mile-long, tree-lined avenue. The park, more interesting than the façade of the house, was full of exotic plants and trees, and ran into the Mahim hills and woods, which so charmed Lady Canning that she compared them to a combination of the palm house at Kew and the setting of *Swiss Family Robinson*.

The house grew in a fairly piecemeal way but it was spacious, with long verandahs, a banqueting hall, and a ballroom, both the latter more than eighty feet long. When Mountstuart Elphinstone took over as Governor in 1819, he enhanced the great rooms with magnificent chandeliers and even introduced furniture in the then avant-garde Egyptian style.

Although Parell was abandoned as a government building so early on, becoming a centre for medical research, it is important in that it demonstrates many of the ways in which the British liked to live in their positions of state power.

Railways, steamships, and the opening of the Suez Canal increased Bombay's importance as the Gateway to India. Visiting royalty and the Viceroy would stay at Parell on their way to Calcutta or Delhi. Fêtes and parties made the house and park into a magical palace: Lady Canning again was particularly enchanted by the long, muslin-draped balconies, the servants dressed in scarlet and gold, and every tree in the grounds illuminated by rush-lights. The most glorious time for the house was the visit in 1875 of Albert Edward, Prince of Wales. Parell was not large enough for the royal retinue, and a camp had to be built in the park to house them. All the chandeliers were lit for the Prince, and a silver throne was made for him to receive the homage of the Princes of India. A crimson carpet woven with the royal coat of arms was spread before the throne, and behind the Prince hung a huge portrait of his mother, Queen Victoria, just in case there should be any doubt as to the proper object of all this gorgeous display.

At the time of the Prince's visit to Bombay, India had already begun to feel the impact of the Gothic Revival. It arrived in the 1860s, and, under the influence of Ruskin, Pugin and Scott, was to be deployed for public buildings as well as for churches. It was the Governor from 1862 to 1867, Sir Bartle Frere, who really brought the Gothic style to Bombay with a vengeance. At a lecture he gave in London in 1870 he was pretty depressing about the activities of the British builders: 'The whole of what the English Government has done for the adornment of the capitals of India may be summed up by saying that very few public buildings have been erected which would be considered at any small seaport town in the country to be above ordinary merit.' His governorship of Bombay gave him the chance to change things, and he seized it. This was a time of great prosperity for the city: the blockade of the Confederate South during the American Civil War, which gave world prominence to India's cotton trade, brought immense wealth to its principal port. An expansion of the city was planned by James Trubshawe, who bore the distinguished

Opposite *The late nineteenth-century Y.M.C.A. in Madras.*

title of Architect to the Ramparts Removal Committee, Bombay. He also designed several new buildings, his best being the austere Gothic Post Office, a three-storey, verandahed building with two towers, which he designed in collaboration with W. Paris. Gothic worked well in Bombay because of the climate, which made it possible to build the kind of southern Italian Gothic that was not suited to the dreary English climate. It was also a part of India rich in good building materials. Red, blue and buff sandstones and basalts were all available, making lively polychromy possible. New work began under the inspiring influence of Lockwood Kipling, who was Professor of Sculpture at the Bombay School of Art, and trained Indian sculptors and carvers to produce fine foliated capitals and decorative work that is still remarkable today.

Under the influence of designs for London's Law Courts and Government Offices, relatively unknown figures designed equivalent structures for Bombay. Col. H. St Clair Wilkins (1828–1896), who was an aide-de-camp to Queen Victoria, designed the Bombay Public Works Office and the Bombay Secretariat, while another military man,

Lieut-Col. James Augustus Fuller (1828–1902), designed the Law Courts in an almost Venetian Gothic style. Bombay's most distinguished public building is the University, built by the Bombay sappers from designs sent out by Sir Gilbert Scott, probably the most distinguished English architect of his day. It is a magnificent and little-known example of his work, entirely Gothic and dominated by the University Library with its gigantic Rajabai Tower, a fascinating illustration of Scott's scholarly approach to architecture. The tower itself is a completed version of the Giotto design for the campanile in Florence. The whole of the University, with its open staircases and wide balconies, would be at home in Italy. Much better known than Scott's work is the Victoria Terminus of the Great India Peninsular Railway by Frederick William Stevens (1848–1900), a huge Indo-Gothic sculptured pile. Opposite the station is the Municipal Building, also by Stevens. A blend of Venetian Gothic and Indo-Saracenic, topped by a tower with a huge dome, these offices for the Bombay Corporation, completed in 1893, are by far the grandest town hall in India.

The character of Bombay is decidedly European,

Public Works Office, Bombay, designed by Henry St Clair Wilkins and begun in 1869. It is an essay in Venetian Gothic, unfortunately partially obscured by mature trees, as are the best buildings of this period. They do, however, survive.

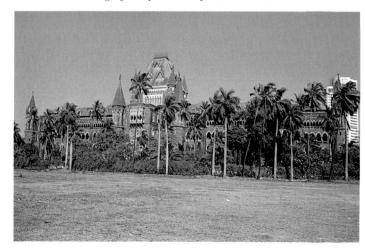

*Victoria Terminus, Bombay. Designed by Frederick William Stevens
and built between 1878 and 1887, it is the
finest Victorian Gothic building in India.*

although there are the beginnings of a blending of indigenous and British Victorian styles. The hill stations, too, feel decidedly British. Eight thousand feet up in the Himalayas is the little hill station of Simla, which in 1864 became the official summer capital. There is a town hall and a library, both half-timbered in a kind of Surrey Tudor. The only major building to be erected in Simla was the Viceregal Lodge, put up between 1884 and 1888. It was designed by Henry Irwin for the Marquis of Dufferin and Ava, and is an uninspiring, grey stone Elizabethan-style house. It looks

St George's School, Hyderabad.

and feels like a hotel in Peeblesshire. Inside, the Viceroys entertained in a suite of Jacobean-type rooms, ideally suited to performances of Gilbert and Sullivan. The Viceroy himself sat at his desk in an elevated turret with a glorious view of the snow-capped peaks of the Himalayas.

Colonel Sir Swinton Jacob (1841–1917), a contemporary of Robert Fellowes Chisholm, was another distinguished advocate of the use of native styles. As a surveyor and engineer he worked for Jaipur State and the Indian Public Works Department, and was responsible for an enormous number of public buildings. Many are in Lucknow, but he particularly encouraged the training of Indian draughtsmen and architects, and built in the native states of Jodhpur, Bhopal and Jaipur.

Vivian Esch (1876–1950) was another architect who developed his own brand of architecture influenced by the Orient. He worked principally for the Nizam of Hyderabad. In the city of Hyderabad his Osmania General Hospital, High School, High Court and Town Hall are all rich in oriental detail. He was an early user of reinforced concrete, and had great confidence, quite rightly, in his trained Indian workforce, saying, 'We can teach the master-craftsman of India very little; on the contrary, we can learn much from him.'

In Calcutta, however, the story was different. The city retained a real faith in the Classical European tradition, and was not alone in this: throughout the length and breadth of India there are simple vernacular Classical buildings that follow the inherited colonial style of the eighteenth century. There can be no doubt that this simple style of verandahs,

OPPOSITE *Prince of Wales Museum, Bombay, built in 1905 and designed by George Wittet. A committed orientalist, he was also responsible for Bombay's Gateway of India.*

A nineteenth-century painting of Government House, Calcutta. It was designed by Lieutenant Charles Wyatt of the Bengal Engineers, and built 1799-1803 at a cost of £63,291. The plan is an adaptation of Kedleston Hall, Derbyshire.

columns and stuccoed brick walls was practical in the Indian climate. But it was seen by the Victorians as insufferably dull. As Lockwood Kipling said, 'There are hundreds of such buildings in India, where, cut up into larger or shorter lengths, they serve for law courts, schools, municipal halls, *dak* bungalows, barracks, post offices, and other needs of our high civilization.' Dull they may have been, but they served their purpose and, I suspect, show the natural level of British taste.

There were, however, high points of British Classical building in India, and the most important example is Government House, Calcutta, adapted by Lieut. Charles Wyatt of the Bengal Engineers from the design of Kedleston Hall in Derbyshire, and built for the Marquis of Wellesley. Like Kedleston, Calcutta's Government House has a central block flanked by four pavilions, linked by curved colonnades to the imposing central portico. It is built of brick and plaster, reminiscent of Nash. The great ceremonial staircase, which is indoors at Kedleston, has been moved to the outside, facing north, and here there are two floors of state rooms, while Kedleston has one. It is a very agreeable house, in a large garden on the Esplanade, and was designed to make a noble impression. It was much criticized for its high cost (Lord Wellesley was building at Barrackpore too), but it was also defended. Lord Valentia saw the point of it: 'I wish', he said in 1803, 'India to be ruled from a Palace, not from a counting house; with the ideas of a Prince, not with those of a retail-dealer in muslins and indigo.' Houses of the British Residents in the native states adopted the same principle, that power had to be wielded with an element of pomp and display, though at Hyderabad the British Resident met considerable opposition from the rich Nizams in matters of display.

The Victoria Memorial in Calcutta, commissioned by Lord Curzon, celebrated this regime. Begun in 1906, and not completed until 1921, it was designed by the then President of the Royal Institute of British Architects, Sir William Emerson, and its construction was supervised by Vivian Esch. Lord Curzon had decreed the style: 'In Calcutta – a city of European origin and construction –

Government Offices, Calcutta, dating from the late nineteenth century. The administration buildings in Calcutta remain largely unchanged to this day.

where all the main buildings have been erected in a quasi-Classical, or Palladian, style, and which possesses no indigenous architectural type of its own – it was impossible to erect a building in any native style ... It was self-evident that a structure in some variety of the Classical or Renaissance style was essential, and that a European architect must be employed.'

The Victoria Memorial, Calcutta, completed in 1921 to a design by Sir William Emerson. The building still dominates the city and was one of the great symbols of Empire in India.

The result is not very happy, but it impresses by the acreage of its marble cladding, the height of the dome with its revolving three-ton figure of Victory, and the heavy atmosphere of imperial nostalgia pervading the collection of exhibits that tell the story of the British occupation of India. In front of the north entrance is a very fine statue of Queen Victoria by Sir George Frampton.

It was the momentous announcement by the King-Emperor George V, at the Delhi Coronation Durbar in 1911, that the capital of India was to be moved from Calcutta to Delhi that marked the high point and ultimate end of British building in India. Sir Edwin Lutyens was first approached to advise on the design of the city in January of 1912, and in April of that year he set sail for India to meet the two other members of the Delhi Planning Commission, Captain G.S.C. Swinton and John A. Brodie. Brodie was the City Engineer for Liverpool, Swinton the Chairman-elect of the London County Council. They surveyed the possible sites for the new city from the back of an elephant. They were looking for ten square miles to build a town to house thirty thousand people. With the words of the Viceroy, Lord Hardinge of Penshurst, in their ears, 'That one Avenue should lead to Purana Kila [the walled, sixteenth-century Muslim city] and another to the Jumma Masjid', it was soon possible to conceive of the city's being built on an equilateral, hexagonal plan. The basis was soon settled, with one principal axis running from the dome of the Viceroy's house on the hill at Raisina to the Jumma Masjid – the Friday Mosque in Shahjahanabad, the old Mogul city of Delhi – and another axis at sixty degrees to this, stretching to the east. This was to be the Rajpath-Kingsway, New Delhi's equivalent to the Washington Mall. When Sir Herbert Baker arrived in Delhi to assist Lutyens he convinced everyone of the advantage of siting both the Viceroy's house and the Secretariats on the eminence. It was agreed from the beginning that Lutyens should design the Viceroy's house and mastermind the entire plan. Baker was to design the Secretariats, deploying his similar experience in South Africa.

To find an acceptable style was a problem in the planning of the new capital. Considerable pressure was exerted on Lutyens by the Indian Government and the Public Works Department to include Indian elements in his designs, but he himself was conviced that the city should be a product of Western humanism, and far from convinced that there actually was an Indian architectural tradition. 'Personally, I do not believe there is *any* real Indian architecture or any great tradition. There are just spurts by various mushroom dynasties with as much intellect as there is in any other *art nouveau*.' In time, he was to change his mind a little, though he could never accept the seeming chaos of the Hindu style. Lutyens was sent off by the Viceroy to look at Indian architecture. He admired the Palace at Dattia, and particularly liked the city of Akbar, Fatehpur-Sikri. It was the synthesis achieved at Akbar which Lutyens emulated in New Delhi – and what he finally achieved was a perfect marriage of Mogul, Hindu and Western elements. He would not for a moment contemplate the use of the Mogul pointed arch, since, for him, the arch was always based on the circle: 'One cannot possibly tinker with the round arch. God did not make the Eastern rainbow pointed to show his wide sympathies.' Lutyens, unlike Baker, was always able to see that there are two ways to build. One way is to mix styles and influences – building 'in fancy dress', as he called it – or you could build as 'an Englishman dressed for the climate'. It is in Lutyens' ordered, austere, splendid Viceroy's house that the synthesis he strove for is made manifest. It is a palace: six hundred and thirty feet wide and five hundred and thirty feet long from west to east, it is bigger even than Versailles. It has Rajput and Mogul qualities. It is predominantly horizontal but dominated by the great dome, a hundred and sixty-six feet above the forecourt. The dome is the essence of New Delhi. The writer and critic Robert Byron described it best of all in 1931: 'Its individuality, its difference from every dome since the Pantheon and particularly from the domes adjoining, lies in its intrinsic solidity. It has the character of a pure monument. Encircled with a narrow gallery, whose function is only to provide, by its blind shadow, a black and further solidifying variant to the red and white, it seems not to have been built, but to have been poured compact from a mould, impermeable to age, destined to stand for ever, to watch the rise of an eighth Delhi and a hundredth Delhi ... [It] recalls the architectural intentions of Antiquity, of Egypt, Babylon, and Persia ...'

It is clear that for one critic, at least, Lutyens had achieved what he set out to do. He succeeded in New Delhi by creating an architecture that has about it the spirit of both East and West. How strong his use is of the *chujja*, the projecting cornice of thin stone taken from the Moguls. How different are Baker's Secretariats – powerful enough on their eminence but feeble in their use of applied native-style decoration. In the circular Parliament building, Baker's enthusiasm for bogus heraldry and the worthy motto almost undermines the intelligence of his planning.

Lutyens designed the interior and garden of the Viceroy's house with brilliance. To arrive by car at the Staircase Court for an evening reception is a moving experience. You climb the stairs into a great stone room which has a coved cornice but no ceiling – only the Indian sky lit by stars, and that imperial dome. Lutyens' use of flowing water throughout the centre of the city reaches its peak both in the Mogul garden, with its water-lily fountain, and on the roof of the Viceroy's house, where inverted domes flow with splashing water. Economies prevented him from covering his buildings with marble, but Lutyens did extract the highest quality of workmanship and stone-cutting from the Indian labourers. The city is also a monument to them.

Other Lutyens buildings in the city include the two smaller palaces for Indian princes – Baroda and Hyderabad – a number of official bungalows and the Public Records Office, and, of course, all the memorials and the great All-India Arch. Henry A.N. Medd designed the two cathedrals in the Classical style. A.G. Shoosmith designed the remarkable brick garrison church.

New Delhi took nineteen years to build, and was occupied by the British for only sixteen years. However, it continues to flourish, and the more everyday buildings by R.T. Russell (Chief Architect to the Government of India from 1919 to 1939), such as the Law Courts, bungalows, Connaught Place, and the shopping centre, are all equally loved and used. It is no small tribute to Lutyens and Baker that all their government buildings in New Delhi are still in use, and are enjoyed by the Government of the Republic. Gandhi's suggestion that the Viceroy's house should become a hospital has never been taken up: it is far too agreeable a residence.

New Delhi's hour of triumph was in 1931 when the new capital was inaugurated with much ceremony. Edward Hudson, a friend and client of Lutyens and the editor of *Country Life*, was so moved by the greatness of the city that he wept, and said to Lady Emily Lutyens: 'Poor old Christopher Wren could never have done this.'

In complete contrast, however, British occupation and government of Burma was troubled and difficult. It is hard today to see what is left of the buildings of the Raj. The first British Resident was, reluctantly, allowed to live in Rangoon in 1829, but it was not until the 1880s that the British occupied Mandalay and the Burmese King and Queen were despatched to India, where they died, near Bombay, in 1916. The Chinese always considered that they had suzerainty over the country, and not until 1886 was a convention signed in Peking that recognized British rule of Burma. The climate of the country claimed many victims, and the earliest architecture, of wood with extensive verandahs open to the breezes, was the healthiest.

In Rangoon some of the public buildings were erected in the Chinese style, but the terrible damage inflicted by the Japanese between 1942 and 1945 has meant that most of the government buildings have been replaced.

In Ceylon, the architecture of Colombo inevitably came under the influence of India, and the earliest Dutch-influenced buildings have largely disappeared. The principal government buildings were put up by the Public Works Department and the survivors are principally Classical in spirit. The Law Courts have a marked resemblance to the Mint in Calcutta. The Parliament building is 1928 Neo-Classical with a porticoed entrance at the top of an impressive flight of steps. The chamber itself follows the Westminster model. The Town Hall, domed and columned,

ABOVE *The All-India War Memorial in New Delhi,
completed in 1931*

LEFT *The Military Barracks, Delhi. Built in the
heart of the Red Fort, the buildings overshadow the old
imperial quarters. They are still in use today.*

was designed by Herbert Reid of Edwards, Reid and Begg, who built a large number of banks and smaller public buildings throughout southern and central India. Colombo Town Hall was built in 1936. The Secretariat is much larger, built of brick and stucco and columned, with cool verandahs along the length of its façade. Built in the mid-1930s, it is still reminiscent of the long Law Courts buildings by Russell in New Delhi. More exotic is the Victoria Memorial Eye Hospital in the Indo-Saracenic style. The Dutch Governor's Residence and the later British Governor-General's house are unexceptional, though well positioned near the harbour.

Palmerston was not very impressed by Hong Kong: 'A barren island with hardly a house upon it', he said in 1853. It was in 1841 that British sovereignty was proclaimed, but the place was always seen as a trading station. The first town, Victoria, had some of the earliest public buildings, but they have mostly disappeared. Government House is still there, and is very ordinary. The oldest part dates from 1853, and it is a plain, two-storey, Neo-Classical building with the ubiquitous verandahs. Hong Kong City Hall of 1869 is stone-built and devoid of any interest – and certainly had no Chinese influence. The 1910 Government Offices, with a tall central clocktower, are in a pleasingly free Edwardian Classical style.

The 1903 Law Courts, probably the best public building in the colony, was designed by Aston Webb and Ingress Bell and described at the time as being

of the English school with details of a Greek character. It is a fifteen-bay long main façade with Ionic columns and a large central dome rising above a pediment. It is a grand granite building with rather pious sculptures of Mercy, Truth, and Justice – Justice being by far the largest figure.

Palmer and Turner were the leading Hong Kong architects in the 1920s and 1930s, and they evolved the kind of inter-war Imperial Classical style for banks and the Hong Kong Club. There is no influence of either Chinese or Portuguese styles in Hong Kong, unlike nearby Macao.

When Sir Stamford Raffles founded Singapore in 1819 he had a pretty clear idea of what it should look like. To begin with, the military built what was necessary for defence, and the Royal Engineers began to lay out plans for the city. But Raffles was lucky: he was joined in 1826 by George Drumgoole Coleman, an architect from Ireland who had been working in India. It was Coleman and Raffles who planned the town, with different areas for the Chinese, Malays, Indians, Arabs and Europeans, divisions that have had a long-lasting influence on Singapore. Raffles determined the width of plots and roads and issued detailed instructions, and Coleman used convict labour to lay out the centre of the town. The early style for everything in Singapore was a skilful adaptation of Palladianism to suit the tropics. The Raffles Institution, built by Coleman between 1836 and 1841, is a delightful, whitewashed simplified Georgian house, somewhat inflated for use as a school.

Singapore's independence from India came about as the East India Company was wound up in 1858. Government House was begun in 1868 by Major J.F. McNair of the Madras Artillery. Between 1864 and 1865 the last public office building for the colony, the Court House, was designed. The Federation of Malay States came into existence in 1895.

The Resident General of the Federation then lived at Carcosa, in Kuala Lumpur, a powerful-looking house well situated in a park. Probably the last Imperial Classical building in the tropics was the Supreme Court, built between 1936 and 1939 by the architect F. Dorrington Ward. There were powerful Indo-Saracenic buildings in Selangor; the Secretariat in the 'Pedang' in Kuala Lumpur was a good example of these influential buildings, which were almost moral in their architectural rectitude.

The Union of South Africa was the third largest of the five self-governing Dominions of the British Empire. Much of the history of the divisions between the Dutch and British settlers is written in the architecture. The four provinces, Natal, the Orange Free State, the Transvaal and the Cape,

The elegant Municipal Council buildings in Penang, Malaysia.
Many of the principal colonial buildings of Penang
are intact and remarkably well preserved.

*City Hall, Kuala Lumpur, 1894–7. Kuala Lumpur's administrative
buildings were built within a decade, which
gives them a unity unusual in England.*

are architecturally distinct.

Around the Cape there are traditional Dutch houses which were later to influence the architecture of Herbert Baker and his patron, Cecil Rhodes. Not until 1814 did the British formally and permanently occupy the Cape, and not until 1910 was the Act of Union passed that united South Africa and made necessary the erection of the Union Buildings of South Africa at Pretoria – probably the best-known manifestation of the imperial presence in Africa.

It was in South Africa that Herbert Baker and Cecil Rhodes really started the whole idea of the establishment of an imperial style of architecture. The relationship between Baker and Rhodes is the most interesting aspect of the South African imperial architectural story. Baker went to South Africa in 1892, aged thirty. He admired Rhodes, the empire builder, and through him he met Kipling and immersed himself in the imperial ideals. Rhodes also introduced Baker to the Cape Dutch domestic architecture of the colony, previously disparaged as the work of inferior Boers. Rhodes asked Baker to rebuild Groote Schuur, which is still the Cape residence of the Prime Minister. Rhodes' respect for cultural roots led him to take a tour of the Mediterranean and then to send his architect protégé on a similar tour. Baker absorbed the imperial message of classical Greece and Rome and returned to develop his style for South Africa. Rhodes died before he and Baker could fulfil their ambitions, and the first achievement of the new style was a memorial to him on the slopes of Table Mountain, with giant steps, flanked by lions, leading up to a columned temple containing a bust of him.

It was Smuts who commissioned Baker to build the Union buildings in Pretoria: he had been impressed by his design

ABOVE *General Post Office, Kuala Lumpur, 1894–7.*

OVERLEAF *City Hall, Cape Town, built in 1905
to a design by Reid and Green.*

Public Library, East London, South Africa, designed by
Page and Cordeaux and built in 1905.

for Pretoria station. Baker saw the advantage of a hillside site and proposed and built two great blocks of official buildings and a linking curved amphitheatre between, where the symbolic union of the English and Dutch races was to take place. Columned loggias were intended by Baker to lure the ministers from their offices so that they could 'lift up their eyes to the high veld'. It was a short-lived vision. South Africa is well supplied with public and civic buildings, but there is little of major importance. H.S. Greave's Parliament House in Cape Town is based on the New Admiralty buildings in London. Parliament House in Pietermaritzburg, Natal, by Barnes and the Public Works Department, is strictly Classical with a very grand portico.

The City Hall in Durban has a look of Edwardian grandeur. It is by Scott Woolcott and Hudson – good, solid, municipal splendour. There are plenty of heavy and ugly town halls in South Africa, and the work of Baker – government buildings at Bloemfontein and his Supreme Courts at Johannesburg – are outstanding by comparison. Lutyens' Art Gallery and Memorial in the same city are of a high, decent, Classical standard.

East Africa is not the richest territory for public buildings,

Supreme Court, Von Brandis Square, Johannesburg, designed by
Baker and Associates and built in 1911.

although a Public Works Department was erected in Mombasa in 1896. Herbert Baker built State House, Mombasa, and the Law Courts in Nairobi, as well as Government House in Nairobi. These extraordinary Mombasa municipal buildings have been described as being in the 'Tudor Baroque' style.

In West Africa there is an almost standard type of Governor's residence, with three storeys, to be found in Bathurst in the Gambia, in Lagos and Nigeria, and its influence is felt in the buildings of Accra and Freetown. Christianborg Castle is the one rather exceptional building on the west coast.

Legislative Council Building, Pietermaritzburg, built c 1898
by the Public Works Department to a design by A. E. Dainton.

Kitchener's plans for the rebuilding of Khartoum, in the Sudan, after the Battle of Omdurman were ambitious, with a series of rectangles where the streets formed the pattern of the Union Flag. It almost followed some of the advanced Garden City ideas. There was a large Governor's Palace, U-shaped in plan, with round-arched galleries.

Such far-flung dominions as Australia and New Zealand carry between them quite a heavy load of British public buildings, without any great architectural achievements. Architecture in both countries has become more interesting as the direct British influence has declined.

Australia's early life as a penal colony means that its imperial architecture dates back to 1788. Some of the simple Classical architecture of this period survives in Tasmania.

In the early nineteenth century Governor Macquarie appointed the first government architect at a salary of three shillings a day. Until the 1840s there was little architectural scholarship, but then the country really began to build and 'the cement of the Victorian age swept over the country like a pestilence'.

Parliament House in Sydney (1811–16) is a simple Classical building with verandahs. Government House in Sydney is a very agreeable castellated Tudor-style house, designed in 1845 by Blore, and the later Town Hall is in the florid Renaissance Colonial Clocktower style.

All the states of Australia had their own Parliament buildings. In 1856, Victoria in South Australia held a competition for a design for theirs, which was won by E.W.

*The Old Market, Mombasa: a rare survivor
among early commercial buildings.*

OPPOSITE *The High Court in Mombasa, 1902.
The Capitol was transferred to Nairobi in 1907
and the High Court after the First World War.*

144

Wright and Lloyd Taylor. Between 1865 and 1868 Charles Tiffin, the architect of Queensland, built his state's Parliament House, and in 1890 Western Australia accepted a design for a Parliament building from J.H. Grainger.

Not until 1908 did the Commonwealth of Australia Royal Commission decide on a site for the building of a federal capital for the nation. Canberra was chosen and an international competition for designs for the new city was held. In 1912 Walter Burley Griffin, the Chicago architect, was announced the winner. The scale of Canberra was to be monumental – a city of twenty-five square miles for a population of 75,000, with room for growth. Griffin based his plan carefully on the topography. An axis aligned to Mount Ainslie led to the two hills for the Parliament and the Capitol. A water axis led from Black Mountain via a series of formal waterways to a large, artificially created lake. Three

centres – federal, municipal and mercantile – linked by radial avenues, followed 'Beaux-Arts' principles. The symbolic centre was the Capitol, a central hill above the Parliament, intended to house a centre of Australian achievements. More democratic than Lutyens, Griffin was prepared to allow 'all forms of aesthetic endeavour'.

Trouble dogged the Canberra plan, and Griffin was sacked in 1920. A Federal Commission was set up to take over, and very little building was accomplished until after 1945. A provisional Parliament was built, and only now is a final building going up.

Australia's native architecture is only just beginning to flourish as she shakes off the influence of imported styles. The mass of public buildings in Melbourne, Sydney, Hobart and Adelaide are not outstanding: all are largely derived from poor European models. The finest achievements are

Custom House, Launceston, Tasmania, designed by
John Lee Archer and built c 1840–50.

Albert Hall, Launceston, Tasmania. Civic pride extended as far as people could travel – particularly in Australia.

original building. It is in these memorials that Australia comes closest to the 'imperial' spirit.

The origins of New Zealand architecture are clearly based on the imported ideals from Britain that travelled with the first settlers. Auckland was founded in 1844, and Government House was its first major construction. Designed by William Mason in 1856, it is simple wooden Classical trying to look like stone. Canterbury was settled by emigrants from England who seem to have had an enthusiasm for the Gothic Revival movement. B.W. Mountfort was the architect of the Provincial Council Buildings at Christchurch (1865), and the High Victorian Gothic interior of the Council Chamber is of excellent quality. The country's Parliament in Wellington by W.H. Clayton must have looked an enormous Classical edifice when it was erected in 1876. It is a dignified and grand wooden building with a good Doric entrance and handsome interior.

Auckland has a few Edwardian public office buildings of some weight, and in Napier there is the fine Greek-style Public Trust office by Hyland and Phillips. The police station in Dunedin, built by the government architect John Campbell, is based on the style of Shaw and Nesfield and is a good example of antipodean Queen Anne style.

The public buildings of the British Empire are exactly what you would expect to have been produced by an Empire that grew at random and which was initially far more concerned with business than politics. The mixed bag of buildings (with one or two notable exceptions) give an insight into the British character. This was not an empire based on cruel repression or tyranny; it was an empire that brought order and a version of democracy to all corners of the globe. Like democracy itself, the architecture of the Empire is understated, uncertain, and often even philistine and bad. Occasionally the Empire (or parts of it) was run by men with vision who wanted to impose their personalities or views. By and large, it is a *laissez-faire* collection of public monuments, too diverse to be considered to share a style or even an aesthetic influence. An easy, tolerant muddle of architecture is what the British have left around the world – much the same as they built for themselves at home.

some of the glorious memorials to the gallant Australians who died for the British Empire in the Great War. The Shrine of Remembrance in Sydney is one of the most complex and beautiful of all First World War memorials. The shrine at Melbourne (1927–33), with its columned portico and stepped pyramidal roof, is a very evocative and

Church Architecture
Gavin Stamp

SIMLA, the summer capital of British India, eight thousand feet up in the foothills of the Himalayas, is a bizarre and exotic place, neither really Indian nor European in character. Yet the presence at the end of the Mall, next to a half-timbered library, of a Gothic Revival church, with buttresses, steeple and pinnacles, such as would look quite at home in Wales or Cornwall, does not strike the visitor as incongruous. It is what he expects. Churches all over the British Empire look like churches back home. They were intended to look familiar, if not nostalgic. By their conventional, reassuring forms they proclaim their function, for a close association exists in Britain between architectural style and religion. Of all the types of building erected in the Empire, churches are the most predictable in style and the least modified from original home prototypes. Such modifications as there may be are usually the product of local

Christ Church, Simla, built 1844–57 to a design by Colonel J. T. Boileau.

conditions and an imperfect memory of the home model in mind.

Churches and chapels are also one of the most numerous of building types throughout the Empire. The fragmentation and division into sects which was such a conspicuous feature of Christianity in Britain soon transferred itself to distant parts of the world and, as soon as means were available, each congregation built itself its own place of worship. A typical colonial city might well have first an Anglican church, probably Classical in style, and later a cathedral, usually Gothic, a Wesleyan Methodist chapel – Greek Revival, possibly – and a Scottish Presbyterian chapel in crude Gothic with lancet windows, perhaps a pre-fabricated structure of corrugated iron. The Roman Catholic church would probably be Romanesque or Italian in style. All the buildings would look as if they had been transplanted from Britain.

In so short a space as this chapter, only a superficial survey can be made of the huge number of places of worship erected in the British Empire before the mid-twentieth century, and it will concentrate on the most prominent and characteristic examples. Inevitably, Anglican buildings must dominate at the expense of churches of other denominations.

With the exception of the more interesting and original designs of the twentieth century, church buildings through-out the Empire derive broadly from two models. The first, which was dominant until the early nineteenth century, was the style of James Gibbs and, in particular, the church of St Martin-in-the-Fields, which is one of the most influential and imitated buildings in architectural history. The solution Gibbs produced for the architectural expression of Anglican worship in London – a galleried, rectangular hall with both a portico and a steeple – was, despite the solecism of having the steeple rise illogically out of the pediment of the portico, soon adopted in America and became the model for most Anglican churches in India. This solution was adopted not as a result of first-hand knowledge of St Martin's but because the designs were published in 1728 in *A Book of Architecture* and so could be reproduced, in however crude a

St Martin-in-the-Fields, London:
the most copied church in the world.

St Andrew's, Madras, designed by Thomas
Fiott de Havilland. Finished in 1820, it is
one of the finest churches in India.

form, by any colonial builder or craftsman with the volume in his possession. Gibbs' book also contained several ideal, unexecuted designs for churches. One of these, circular in plan, provided the model for St Andrew's Church, Madras, completed in 1820.

By this date the conventional Classicism of Gibbs was being sharpened by knowledge of the Greek Revival, but there was also growing up a much more potent influence which would bring the early colonial tradition in ecclesiastical architecture to an end, and, indeed, condemn many Georgian churches to mutilation or demolition. This, the second great source of inspiration for church builders in the Empire, was the Gothic Revival. An antiquarian interest in medieval architecture, combined with the fact that most old

churches and cathedrals in England were Gothic, ensured that new churches back home, built following the Church Building Act of 1818, were in the Gothic style. By the 1840s, thanks to Pugin, the Cambridge Camden Society, and the beginning of the great mid-Victorian religious revival, the conviction was strong that Gothic was the only true Christian style and that Classical churches were not only old-fashioned but pagan in inspiration.

The Gothic Revival soon influenced building in the Empire. By the 1830s crude Gothic chapels were being erected in South Africa and Australia. If less well adapted to hot climates than Classical designs, such churches were probably easier and cheaper to build. They did not need porticos, steeples were optional, and the windows could be

*St Paul's Cathedral, Calcutta, completed in 1847 to a design
by William Nairn Forbes, a military engineer.*

simple lancets. By the 1850s the first archaeologically 'correct' churches, the product of developments in England in the 1840s, were being erected in distant spots thousands of miles from the prototypes whose tracery and pinnacles had been carefully drawn and measured. St John's Cathedral, Newfoundland, and St John's, Colaba, Bombay, are two early examples of this.

These two last buildings also reflected another new attitude to colonial church architecture, for they were the work of professional architects in England. In the eighteenth and early nineteenth centuries, churches in the colonies were almost always designed by amateurs – at best, military engineers. For instance, St John's Church, Calcutta, a version of St Martin-in-the-Fields, consecrated in 1787, was designed by James Agg, a young officer in the Royal Engineers who had gone out to India in 1779 with William Hickey; St Andrew's, Madras, was also the work of an engineer, Thomas de Havilland. Often the name of the 'architect' of a church is obscure and long forgotten. Skinner's Church in Delhi was not, in fact, designed by the cavalry officer, Colonel James Skinner, but by Colonel Robert Smith of the Bengal Engineers, who was also responsible for St George's, Penang. Civilian architects were rare and exceptional before Victoria's reign. One such was G.D. Coleman, who worked in Calcutta and then in Singapore, where he designed the original St Andrew's Church, built between 1835 and 1836. And Sydney was fortunate enough to be able to enjoy the professional skills of

Francis Greenway, who was transported there in 1814, having been convicted of fraud in Bristol. Greenway was responsible for several Neo-Classical churches in New South Wales. More sophisticated architecture arrived early in Tasmania, thanks to John Lee Archer, an Irish, London-trained engineer and architect.

The high seriousness of the Gothic Revival, combined with an expanding imperial vision, put an end to this comparative amateurism. By the mid-nineteenth century colonial bishops were anxious to secure the services of notable architects. Following the burning of his old cathedral, the Bishop of Newfoundland came back to England in 1846 and secured plans for a new Gothic building from George Gilbert Scott. By the 1860s William Burges had been commissioned to supply designs for Brisbane Cathedral, R.C. Carpenter for Colombo Cathedral, and William Butterfield for Adelaide Cathedral. Such projects were enthusiastically described by that partisan of serious Gothic, A.J.B. Beresford Hope, in his book of 1861, *The English Cathedral of the Nineteenth Century*, in which he discussed two possible adaptations of Gothic to hot climates: the 'draught-admitting' and the 'speluncar', or massive and cave-like. Unfortunately, few of the designs of these accomplished ecclesiastical architects were ever erected as they would have wished, for the plans were often found to be impractical or too expensive when they eventually arrived,

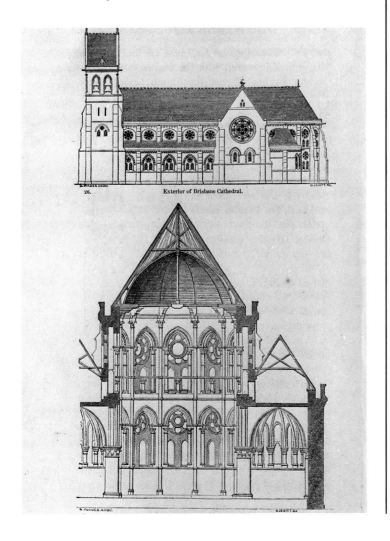

Exterior of Brisbane Cathedral.

LEFT *Brisbane Cathedral, commissioned from William Burges in 1859 but finally built by J. L. Pearson in 1901.*

A design for the interior of an 'iron pot' church.

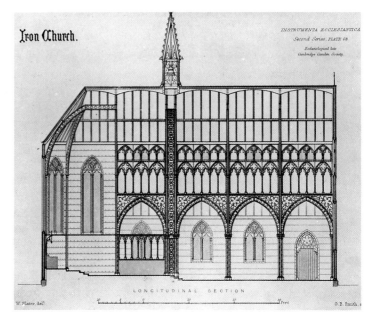

Iron Church.

INSTRUMENTA ECCLESIASTICA
Second Series. PLATE 68.

LONGITUDINAL SECTION

152

and were either abandoned or modified by local architects in response to local conditions.

Many colonial churches were designed as temporary structures and were often assembled from prefabricated parts made in Britain and shipped out. This is a mysterious area of architectural history, as yet little investigated. Early nineteenth-century prefabricated churches were of timber; later ones – 'iron pot' churches or 'tin tabernacles' – had either an iron frame or walls of corrugated iron. Manufactured in Britain, they were advertised for export to the colonies, though they were not always as useful as their designers supposed. In Adelaide in 1838 the building committee for the Anglican church decided to discard the prefabricated structure sent out from England and build a church in stone instead. In the same year, the Wesleyans in Adelaide sold their prefabricated chapel to the Quakers, who re-erected it elsewhere in the town. Similar structures were sometimes used by the Roman Catholics in Scotland, and examples used by Nonconformist congregations may still be found in Britain. It was, presumably, with the colonies in mind that the Ecclesiological Society, normally so hostile to iron architecture, commissioned William Slater to design an 'iron church'. His plans were published in the second edition of *Instrumenta Ecclesiastica* in 1856, and the plates suggest that Slater envisaged a prefabricated iron structure faced in corrugated metal.

Before the twentieth century very few architects had qualms about importing purely British types of architecture into exotic, distant lands (Colonel Richard Pilkington, who designed Gibraltar Cathedral in the Moorish style in the 1820s, was an exception).

John Oldrid Scott, second son of Sir Gilbert Scott, never visited India to see either the site for the cathedral which he designed in Lahore, or the completed building; nor did G.F. Bodley ever visit Nagpur or Hobart, where cathedrals were built to his designs. Robert Weir Schultz, having been asked to design a cathedral in Khartoum, did visit the Sudan twice, in 1907 and again in 1912 when the building was consecrated. Adrian Gilbert Scott was first asked to design All Saints' Cathedral in Cairo in 1916, when he was serving in Egypt with the armed forces. Such cases are typical of the last, and in many ways the most interesting phase of ecclesiastical architecture in the British Empire. But by the twentieth century, many architects were anxious not only to adapt European models to local climatic conditions in a pragmatic manner but also to respect indigenous traditions and styles. This was partly a reflection of the Arts and Crafts movement, and partly a product of the general dissatisfaction with literal reproductions of historic styles.

Also by the early twentieth century, travel had become easier, and well-trained, talented architects were often on the spot and ready and able to supervise the erection of sophisticated and imaginative designs. In South Africa, Herbert Baker, having been trained in one of the best offices in London, designed a number of important churches in a sort of Arts and Crafts Gothic adapted to local materials, while in India, two of Lutyens' and Baker's local representatives, Medd and Shoosmith, designed remarkable churches in Delhi, inspired by the Lutyens Classical tradition.

The increasing sophistication of church architecture in the Empire was not merely a product of developing architectural ideas back in Britain and of better and easier communications. It also reflected the development of ecclesiastical organization and the establishment of new dioceses. The encouragement of new dioceses, and the building of cathedrals as a focus of local life and effort within the Church of England overseas, was a product of the Victorian missionary spirit and the purpose behind Beresford Hope's book. The building of churches went hand in hand with the expansion of the diocesan system and the establishment of new self-supporting missions.

In 1786 an act was passed which permitted colonial and missionary bishoprics. Before this date parishes had been established in America and elsewhere, but often the only permanent place of Anglican worship was a garrison church, built by and for the military, and which was sometimes too small for the rest of the local community. It was to encourage the building of churches, the provision of clergy, and the establishment of missions that the Society for the Propagation of the Gospel in Foreign Parts (S.P.G.) was created, by royal charter, in 1701. For the next two centuries, the history of church building in the colonies is, to a great extent, the history of the S.P.G. The Society's munificence was employed to assist local initiatives. By 1741 the S.P.G. had helped to build a hundred churches in America. Individual examples of the Society's help are too numerous to mention, but perhaps the building of the second church at St John's, Newfoundland, in 1800 after the French had burnt the first deserves note. The S.P.G. donated £500 and King George III personally gave £200. In 1820 the S.P.G. voted £2,000 to the Bishop of Quebec for church building; the previous year £5,000 had gone to the Bishop of Calcutta for the same purpose. In 1851 the S.P.G. spent £23,169 in India and supported forty-four missionaries in the four dioceses then covering India, Ceylon, Burma and Malaya. In 1900 its grants to the same area, now divided among eleven dioceses, amounted to £38,820.

The S.P.G.'s work was greatly assisted by the establishment of new bishoprics. Until the creation of the diocese of Calcutta in 1814, money could only be spent on schools in India. Following the 1786 act, the first new Anglican bishoprics outside the British Isles were created, in Canada in 1787 and 1793. Holy Trinity Cathedral, Quebec, another version of St Martin-in-the-Fields begun in 1800, was the second Anglican cathedral to be built since the Reformation (the first being St Paul's, London). In 1835 the new dioceses of Calcutta and Madras were carved out of that of Calcutta, and in 1839 Newfoundland and Bermuda were made dioceses. Throughout the rest of the nineteenth century many more new bishoprics were created, but often their cathedrals were merely upgraded parish churches. The cathedral building movement of Victoria's reign really began in 1838, when Bishop Daniel Wilson decided to build a cathedral in Calcutta. This charming building, the work of an engineer, was later dismissed by strict Gothic Revival-ists but, as Beresford Hope admitted in 1872: 'The lack of means, or the impossibility of providing grandeur or space, is no excuse for postponing the Cathedral. After all, the essentials of a Cathedral are an altar whereat to plead the Christian propitiation, a chair whereon to sit, a font wherein to baptise, and a Bishop to occupy that chair, to plead that propitiation before the altar, and to receive Christ's servants at that font.'

A survey of cathedral churches presented by the late Rev. Basil Clarke in his pioneering book *Anglican Cathedrals Outside the British Isles*, published in 1958, reveals an extraordinarily varied range of buildings: some incomplete, some successively enlarged, some mean, some the executed designs of proper architects, some enchantingly provincial and amateur. As a place of worship was sometimes the first communal building to be erected after the foundation of a colony, the first church was often crude and temporary, and was replaced by a more sophisticated structure as funds and expertise permitted. A typical example of the many early colonial churches was the first one to be erected in Australia. The Rev. Richard Johnson went out to Botany Bay in 1786, and in 1793 he built a primitive church of wattle and daub in the traditional vernacular manner of England. This was rebuilt in 1798 and rebuilt again, as a masonry structure in the Gothic style, in 1848. It is now the Church of St Philip, Church Hill, Sydney.

In the American colony of Virginia a system of parishes was established as early as 1612. St Luke's – the Old Brick Church – Isle of Wight County, Virginia, was built in 1632 and is an example of 'Gothic Survival' such as might have been built in England shortly after the Reformation. It is a remarkable building, but not at all typical of churches built in the colony before the War of Independence. The typical eighteenth-century American church is a provincial adaptation of the designs of Wren and Gibbs, built in brick, wood

OPPOSITE *St Luke's Church, Isle of Wight County, Virginia. Built in 1632, this is the oldest existing church in the United States.*

Bruton Parish Church, Williamsburg, Virginia. It was designed by
Governor Spottiswood on a cruciform plan and built in 1711.

156

The Protestant Episcopal Church of Old Trinity, Church Creek,
Maryland. It was built in 1674 along the lines of
a rustic brick cottage, with an apsidal end.

and plaster. St James's, Goose Creek, South Carolina, of 1713, has round-headed windows, quoins, and simple classical porches in the Wren manner. More sophisticated was the second Bruton Parish Church at Williamsburg, Virginia, designed in 1711 on a Latin cross plan by Governor Spotswood. Similar to this, elegant and very simple, is Christ Church, Lancaster County, Virginia, of 1732.

None of these early American churches sported the steeple which Wren added to his City of London churches. The first to do so was St Philip's, Charleston, South Carolina (now destroyed), of between 1711 and 1723, which had a steeple deriving from Wren's St Magnus the Martyr, which itself was modelled on the Church of St Charles Borromeo in Antwerp. Wren's ideal church for a congregation of 2,000 was St James's, Piccadilly, with its galleried

King's Chapel, Boston, Massachusetts, designed by
Peter Harrison 1749–54. The interior is particularly fine. A spire that he planned
was never built.

interior, brick construction, and simple steeple. This may well have been the model for the Old North Church, Boston, Massachusetts, begun in 1723. Knowledge of Wren's design may possibly have been disseminated by the S.P.G., which raised funds for the building. Soon after this followed the Old South Meeting House in Boston, built by the Congregationalists in 1729–30, with a form similar to the Anglican Old North Church. Another version of St James's, Piccadilly, was Trinity Church, Newport, Rhode Island, built in wood between 1725 and 1741.

Trinity Episcopal Church, Newport, Rhode Island,
built 1725–6 by master carpenter Richard Munday.

Christ Church, Lancaster County, Virginia, built in 1732:
the only Virginian church of the period still with its
original high-backed pews and three-storey pulpit.

Touro Synagogue, Newport, Rhode Island, designed by Peter Harrison and built
in 1759. George Washington wrote to the congregation in 1790 stating that
the country would give 'bigotry no sanction and persecution no assistance'.

However, the most typical American church, with a steeple rising from behind a portico, derives from Gibbs and St Martin-in-the-Fields. A copy of Gibbs' *Book of Architecture* was evidently available to the builders of Christ Church, Philadelphia, begun in 1727. This was completed in 1754 with a steeple modelled on that of St Martin's. Another church inspired by the prototype is St Michael's, Charleston, South Carolina, of between 1752 and 1761, and the twin churches on the green at New Haven, Connecticut. Despite hostility to the Church of England in Nonconformist New England, even the First Baptist Meeting House in Providence, Rhode Island, built just before the Revolution, in 1774–5, has a steeple copied from one of Gibbs' alternative designs for that of St Martin-in-the-Fields.

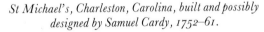

St Michael's, Charleston, Carolina, built and possibly designed by Samuel Cardy, 1752–61.

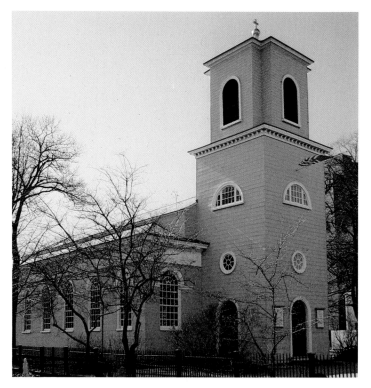

Christ Church, Cambridge, Massachusetts. Designed by Peter Harrison
and built in 1761, it was used during
the Revolution as a barracks for British troops.

The influence of Gibbs on church architecture continued in America, both in the United States and in British Canada, where the diocese of Nova Scotia, the first Anglican diocese created outside the British Isles, was formed in 1787 and that of Quebec in 1793. In Halifax, Nova Scotia, Bishop Inglis had to make do with St Paul's Church, built in 1750 on the model of the simple Georgian brick box, St Peter's, Vere Street, London. In Quebec City, the foundation stone of Holy Trinity Cathedral was laid in 1800. The architects, Captain Hall and Major Robe of the Royal Engineers, modelled their design, needless to say, on St Martin-in-the-Fields, but simplified the details. The interior, with its box pews, galleries, Venetian east window, and coved plaster vault rising above Ionic columns, is a welcome survival and a testimony to the timeless utility of Gibbs' architecture. More splendid, with greater architectural ambitions, is St George's Cathedral, Kingston, Ontario, begun in 1825 to the designs of Rogers. In 1846 it was given a dome rising above transepts. Despite the different dates of construction the interior seems a coherent and impressive essay in Classical architecture. But long before the building was finished in its present form, the Gothic Revival had determined the style of most of Canada's Anglican ecclesiastical architecture.

Possibly owing to the legacy of Spain, the Classical tradition survived longer in the West Indies. St John's

St George's Cathedral, Kingston, Ontario,
begun in 1825.

Cathedral, Antigua, was built between 1845 and 1848, following the destruction of the old church in 1843, the year after the foundation of the diocese. The architect was Thomas Fuller, who created a sober Classical design, rich in 'Gibbs surrounds' and with two west towers. Such a design was very old fashioned by this date: the *Ecclesiologist* dismissed it as, 'A mere overgrown Pagan church, of the old school of St Marylebone and St Philip's, Regent Street, with two dumpy pepper-box towers'.

In the earliest church buildings in British India, the influence of Wren and, in particular, of James Gibbs was also potent, but the results differed from contemporary churches in America. Most Indian churches were of brick construction, faced with *chunam*, or stucco, and, because of the climate, were often provided with deeper and more generous porticos. A typical example is St John's, Calcutta, which for a time served as the cathedral. This, designed by James Agg and built between 1784 and 1787, is rectangular in plan, with interior colonnades, and has a steeple in the Gibbs manner. Within twenty years, the building had been altered to suit the climate, for deep colonnaded verandahs were placed along the long sides. St John's manifests all the considerable charms of Engineer's Classical architecture. If illiterate in detail, it is full of reminiscences of Europe, though its external colonnades seem sensible and appropriate in the heat of India. The interior is cool and spacious, the generous openings for ventilation being filled with pierced screens. The walls are lined with Neo-Classical monuments to the memory of so many officers and traders who lasted but a short time in India before succumbing to the climate. St Andrew's, Calcutta, next to the Writers' Buildings in Dalhousie Square, is a more competent essay on Gibbs' St Martin-in-the-Fields plan, built in 1815.

St Thomas's Church, now Cathedral, Bombay, is the oldest Anglican church in India, and is characteristic of British India. It was begun in 1672 but not completed until 1718. A delightfully crude Gothic west tower was added in 1838 after the building had been raised to the dignity of a cathedral, but, despite the battlements on the walls, and the Victorian chancel, St Thomas's is essentially a Classical building, with irregular, round-headed windows and an interior dominated by large and gauche Doric columns.

In Madras, St Mary's Church within Fort St George was originally built between 1678 and 1680, one of the earliest English churches in India, but it was completely rebuilt in 1759 and is now a simple, stuccoed building with a steeple in the tradition of Wren. St George's Cathedral, Madras, was consecrated in 1816, and is yet another essay on the theme of St Martin-in-the-Fields. It was designed by the engineer James Caldwell, with Thomas de Havilland of the Bengal Engineers being responsible for its erection. The Gibbs prototype is here adapted to the climate by the enthusiastic and undisciplined addition of porticos and verandahs, all with splendid depth and a superfluity of columns, faced, like the whole building, in white *chunam*.

De Havilland was himself responsible for the most interesting church in India on the Gibbs theme. This is St Andrew's Presbyterian Church, Madras, built between 1818 and 1820. To achieve the centralized plan desired by the Nonconformist congregation, de Havilland adopted Gibbs' unexecuted design for a circular church published in his *Book of Architecture*. The building has a giant Ionic order around the whole of the exterior and a particularly fine steeple. The pedimented eastern façade has the familiar proportions of St Martin-in-the-Fields, but the *oeil de boeuf* is flanked by naïvely fierce lions. Another centrally planned church is St James's, Old Delhi – Skinner's Church – designed by Colonel Robert Smith and built between 1828 and 1835. Here there is a Greek cross plan, with each arm terminating in a Doric portico, and above the central

---

OPPOSITE *St James's (or Skinner's) Church, Delhi, designed by Colonel Robert Smith and built in 1828–35 at the sole expense of Colonel James Skinner. It was the scene of fierce fighting in 1857 during the Mutiny.*

octagonal space rises a dome which is more Baroque in inspiration. Neo-Classicism was moving on to Early Victorian richness – but the Gothic Revival would be imported to India soon after.

A similar centralized plan was adopted by the architect George Drumgoole Coleman for the Armenian Church of St Gregory the Illuminator in Singapore. Three of the four arms off the central rectangular space – a traditional Armenian plan – end in generous, deep Doric porticos. The fourth arm now sports an octagonal steeple, added (not by Coleman) between 1849 and 1859. Unfortunately, Coleman's other church in Singapore, St Andrew's, for the Church of England, had been demolished. This, built between 1834 and 1836, was another simple, elegant Doric building in

stucco, but having twice been struck by lightning, it was demolished in 1854 and the present St Andrew's Cathedral is a pedestrian essay on the theme of Netley Abbey, in Hampshire, designed by Captain Ronald McPherson of the Madras Army and built by convicts.

St Andrew's Cathedral, Sydney, was built to a design by the resourceful architect Francis Greenway, the pupil of Nash who had been condemned to death in Bristol for forgery, and then transported to Australia. Pardoned by Governor Macquarie, he designed several public buildings in the colony. St Andrew's Church was begun in 1819 but never completed. In this case Greenway provided a Gothic design but most of his buildings are Neo-Classical, such as St James's, King Street, Sydney, of between 1817 and 1820.

The Armenian Church, Singapore. Built in the 1830s, it is the oldest surviving church in the city.

*Texture and colour rather than design are often the factors
which distinguish the colonial copy from the English original,
as in this church in Kuala Lumpur.*

167

The earliest churches in Tasmania were also designed by an architect with first-hand knowlege of contemporary British architecture. This was John Lee Archer, who had worked for John Rennie, set up as an architect and engineer, and in 1826 took the post of Civil Engineer to the government of Van Diemen's Land. His St David's Church, Hobart, of 1816, gave way to a Gothic Revival Cathedral erected from plans sent out by G.F. Bodley in 1866, but St George's, Battery Point, of between 1836 and 1852, survives, and is a pure essay in the Greek Revival.

The Greek Revival also manifested itself in South Africa, where one of the last tributes was paid to St Martin-in-the-Fields. St Andrew's Presbyterian Church in Cape Town, of between 1827 and 1828, is a Greek Doric building, and the now demolished St George's, Cape Town, was Greek Ionic. Cape Town has, of course, several large and splendid Dutch churches of the eighteenth century. The first Anglican place of worship in South Africa was a warehouse in Simonstown, converted into a church and schoolroom in 1814 by Thibault, the French architect who had formerly worked for the Dutch East India Company. The first permanent church in Cape Town was St George's, built between 1830 and 1834. The architect was Schutte, but the design was closely based on that of St Pancras Parish Church in London, one of the finest Greek Revival buildings in the capital, built between 1819 and 1822 by W. and H.W. Inwood. Plans of this had been secured by Lieut-Col. Bell, Colonial Secretary, in 1829. The building in Cape Town reproduced its Greek Ionic portico and steeple but omitted the caryatid side vestries. St Pancras Church itself is a rectangular, galleried box with portico and steeple, which was essentially Gibbs' plan for St Martin-in-the-Fields rendered into Greek, so St George's, Cape Town, was a late but particularly fine child of that most prolific parent of colonial church buildings. The replacement of old St George's by a new cathedral designed by Herbert Baker was one of the saddest crimes of the Gothic Revival.

One more early Anglican church in South Africa deserves mention. This is St John's, Bathurst, designed by Lieut-Col. Michell and built in 1831. It is a rugged and simple Classical design, almost reminiscent of Vanbrugh. The Rev. William Shaw, who saw it soon after it was built, considered that 'this village church, together with the cluster of surrounding scenery and buildings, serves to remind an Englishman of many a rural spot in his own country of surpassing beauty'. That, of course, was the intention behind the design of so many churches in distant colonies.

Enthusiasm for the Gothic Revival coincided nicely with the cathedral and church building movement of the mid-Victorian decades so that it left its mark on the new colonies then expanding with white settlers. In India, Gothic churches remain slightly incongruous and unusual; in Canada, Australia, and South Africa they are the norm. Architectural fashion, reinforced by the belief in Gothic as the true Christian style, overcame the many practical objections to the style in exotic countries. A Gothic Revival church demands good building stone, which was often not available, whereas a fine Classical church could be made of simple bricks, faced in plaster. Gothic is also a style of northern Europe, and is not easily adapted to hot climates; unlike Classical buildings with generous porticos, the models for Gothic churches do not provide areas of shade and cool. Mid-Victorian architects attempted, therefore, to adapt Gothic in two ways: by enlarging the windows to admit currents of air, or by thickening the walls and making the windows small to produce heat-resisting 'speluncar' buildings. Not surprisingly, the more temperate parts of the Empire saw the more successful essays in Gothic Revival church building.

Most of the Anglican cathedrals in Canada are Gothic, with very English-looking spires. Halifax, Montreal and Toronto Cathedrals are all competent, if pedestrian, mid-Victorian Gothic Revival buildings, all closely following precedent. Canada, indeed, could boast some of the earliest examples of 'correct' archaeological Gothic outside the British Isles. The first Bishop of Fredericton secured the services of Frank Wills, who came to Canada in 1845 and designed a cathedral, based on Snettisham Church, Norfolk, which was begun that same year. Wills went on to the United States, where, in 1850, he published *Ancient English*

Ecclesiastical Architecture, and its Principles applied to the Wants of the Church at the Present Day. The Bishop of Fredericton revisited England to raise money for his cathedral and obtained designs for a central tower and spire from William Butterfield. These were executed and the cathedral was consecrated in 1853.

The Anglican church (made a cathedral in 1839) in St John's, Newfoundland, had the curious distinction of having been burned down three times – once by the French, and twice by accident – and the present fine Gothic Revival building has been worked on by four generations of a great English architectural dynasty. After the burning of the second building, the Bishop of Newfoundland came to England in 1846 to secure plans from a good ecclesiastical

Christ Church Cathedral, Fredericton, New Brunswick, 1845–53.

St James's Cathedral, Toronto, built in 1853.
It has the highest spire in Canada (97 metres).

architect. These were provided by George Gilbert Scott, then a rapidly rising star in the Gothic Revival. Work on his design, which the *Ecclesiologist* thought 'learned and dignified, but perhaps cold', began in 1848 under an experienced English clerk of works. The nave was built first, in the Early English style. Following the death of Scott, George Gilbert Scott Junior was in 1880 entrusted with the completion of the choir, transepts and crossing tower, and he made slight changes to his father's designs. Apart from the tower, work was complete when, in 1892, the building was largely destroyed by fire. The rebuilding to the same design was carried out by G.G. and J.O. Scott, under the superintendence of J.W. Willis, but, as by this date G.G. Scott Junior had become insane, the responsibility was carried by his younger brother. The choir and transepts were reopened in 1895; the nave was not repaired until early this century. Designs for a reredos and for the still incomplete crossing tower were invited from G.G. Scott Junior's son, Giles Gilbert Scott, the architect of Liverpool Cathedral. Scott actually visited Newfoundland in 1920 – the first member of the family to do so. The reredos was carried out but the crossing tower remains unfinished. Designs for finishing parts of the cathedral have been prepared by a fourth generation: Richard Gilbert Scott, whose father, Sir Giles, also designed a fine chapel for Trinity College, Toronto.

The most spectacular Gothic Revival building is not, however, Anglican. Nor is it an example of 'correct' Gothic; indeed, as a pre-Puginian example of the Revival, it represents everything that Beresford Hope and strict ecclesiologists despised. This is the Roman Catholic Church of Notre Dame, Montreal, designed by James O'Donell, an Irish Protestant who had lived in New York and who became a Roman Catholic before he died in Montreal in 1830. The body of the church, replacing a seventeenth-century building, was built between 1823 and 1829, but the two tall west towers were not finished until 1843, and the interior took many decades to decorate and furnish. The interior is extraordinary: a vast space under a blue spangled vault, with two tiers of galleries between the iron columns. The floor slopes gently down towards the dominating pinnacled reredos in the apse, the work of the architect Victor Bourgeau and the sculptor Bouriche, completed in 1878. Around one of the pillars curls an astonishing wooden pulpit – Gothic in detail, but Baroque in inspiration – the work of Bourgeau and the sculptor Philippe Hebert between 1883 and 1885. Throughout, invention and resourcefulness are displayed in departing from strict precedent, but the building is richly embellished with all the colour of the Middle Ages. And with its wide, auditorium-like space, and with light filtering through coloured glass in the vault, Notre Dame Church has both the romantic glamour of Fonthill and the glitter of a twentieth-century atmospheric cinema, such as the Granada, Tooting. It is surely one of the most delightful Gothic Revival churches in the world. The sadness is that the Sacred Heart Chapel, added behind the high altar between 1888 and 1891, has been destroyed by fire.

In Australia, many of the churches and cathedrals are associated with the names of famous English architects, but, as none of the designers ever went out to supervise their work in the nineteenth century, the resulting buildings often look very different from the confidently prepared perspective drawings. William Burges, for instance, designed an early French 'semi-speluncar' cathedral for Brisbane with four-foot thick walls in 1859, but these plans had been dropped by 1867. When a cathedral was eventually begun, on a different site, in 1901, it was to the designs of another distinguished English Gothicist, J.L. Pearson, architect of Truro Cathedral. This remains incomplete, but what was built by 1910 – choir and transepts – is characteristic of the architect: French Gothic in style, and vaulted throughout.

The story of Melbourne Cathedral is slightly happier. The original cathedral church, since rebuilt on another site, was a simple Classical design by Robert Russell, built between 1839 and 1842 by convict labour. A new cathedral was soon demanded as the Gothic Revival became dominant and the province of Victoria expanded. In 1851 there were 39 churches and chapels in the province, and 2,602 twenty years later. (On average five churches a week were opened throughout Queen Victoria's reign.) In 1877, William Butterfield, that austere, harsh master of polychromatic Gothic, architect of Keble College, Oxford, was invited to prepare designs, which were sent out the following year. Samples of local stone were sent to England so that Butterfield could choose the best for the cream-and-grey-banded stonework of walls and pillars. In 1886 Butterfield resigned, and when the cathedral was consecrated in 1891, it had been completed and furnished by Joseph Read, a local architect. Early this century, three spires were added to designs by James Barr of Sydney. The building has, nevertheless, much of the vigour of Butterfield's personal style of Gothic; the interior is reminiscent of Keble College Chapel and St Alban's, Holborn, in London.

Although very English in appearance, with a west front

reminiscent of York Minster, St Andrew's Cathedral, Sydney, was a more indigenous effort not reliant upon drawings shipped from the other side of the world. After Francis Greenway's project had been abandoned, Bishop Boughton began work in 1837 on a fifteenth-century Gothic design based on Oxford precedents. Work stopped in 1842 but resumed in 1846 on a revised design prepared by E.T. Blacket, a young enthusiast for Gothic with no professional training, who had been persuaded to stay in Australia while en route for New Zealand. Blacket, having entered government service, was obliged to resign, and work was continued under T.W. Shepard as clerk of works. The cathedral was

The Anglican church of St Luke's, Richmond, Tasmania. It was built in 1843 to a design by John Lee Archer, who was responsible for half a dozen churches in Tasmania, as well as several other major buildings. He was sacked to make way for the nephew of the Governor.

consecrated in 1868 and the towers completed in 1874. Blacket also designed the cathedrals in Goulburn and Perth.

A more original and appropriate cathedral in Newcastle, the largest in Australia, was begun in 1881 and built in brick, to the designs of John Horbury Hunt of Sydney. The final result, completed by others, has an impressive simplicity. St David's Cathedral in Hobart, Tasmania, has, by contrast, a careful refinement typical of its English architect, G.F. Bodley. It was begun in 1868, but by the time the choir was consecrated in 1894, Bodley had revised his designs and the completed building is typical of his best work, with finely cut stone. The detached tower was not finished until 1936. As Basil Clarke remarked, 'The present tower shows Bodley at his most Bodleian. It is fortunate that the builders of 1936 had the piety to keep to his plans, and not to substitute something contemporary.' Adelaide Cathedral is also English in style, but of a Gothic heavier and earlier in date than Bodley's. William Butterfield had prepared designs in 1847, and the building which was finally begun in 1869 was designed by the local architects Woods and McMinn, who adapted Butterfield's plans.

Early churches in New Zealand were also 'correct' Gothic, chiefly owing to Bishop Selwyn, who had been a member of the Cambridge Camden Society, and who was determined to adapt Gothic to local traditions. As a result, several churches are interesting Gothic designs in wood. In 1841, Selwyn asked the Society to provide him with models for a cathedral in Auckland and for parish churches. His principal architect was Frederick Thatcher, who came out from England in 1843 and who was later ordained. Thatcher was the architect of the (old) cathedral in Wellington, built between 1864 and 1866, of the cathedral in Nelson, built in wood between 1848 and 1858, and of such buildings in the 'Selwyn style' as St John's College Chapel, Auckland.

The other important New Zealand ecclesiastical architect was B.W. Mountfort, who had been a pupil of both R.C. Carpenter and G.G. Scott before emigrating from England in 1850. With such impeccable Gothic credentials, he was well qualified to supervise the construction of Christ Church Cathedral, Christchurch, built between 1864 and 1901 to designs sent out by Scott. Mountfort designed many Gothic churches in New Zealand, such as Napier Cathedral, as well as public buildings.

South Africa was another British colony where the Gothic style was almost exclusively used for Anglican churches. Until its demolition, St George's, Cape Town, was one of the few conspicuous exceptions. In the history of the Gothic Revival in Africa, an important role was played by a remarkable woman, Sophie Gray, the wife of Bishop Gray, who arrived in Cape Town in 1848. The Bishop described his wife as 'architect to the diocese', and Sophie Gray apparently designed many churches herself. She was certainly a competent draughtsman, and had the ability to adapt designs to particular circumstances, her ideas being derived from Rickman's and the Pugins' books on Gothic architecture and the publications of the Ecclesiological Society – which were, indeed, intended for this very purpose. Mrs Gray's plans were submitted to the Surveyor General, Charles Bell, who provided much practical help. Sophie Gray built some two dozen churches in this way before her death in 1871. A good example of her work is St Saviour's Church, Claremont, built in 1850. It is a standard, ecclesiologically 'correct' design, well executed, with a nave and lean-to aisles, a separate chancel, and a western bell-cote, well handled.

Sophie Gray also designed St Mark's Cathedral, George, but perhaps the most interesting building with which she was associated is St Peter's Cathedral, Pietermaritzburg, Natal. Work began on her very simple Gothic design in 1851, but in 1854 Bishop Colenso decided to 'place the original drawings in the hands of some competent architect in England' so that 'correct designs may be furnished for the proposed additions'. Who the 'competent architect' consulted was is not recorded. The church, finished in 1857, had a chancel but no transepts. It was in St Peter's that, in 1866, Dean Green read out the sentence of excommunication on Bishop Colenso for heresy, but the courts allowed Colenso to retain possession of the building. A schism developed, and a new Anglican cathedral, St Saviour's, was begun in 1868.

Colenso's cathedral survives today, next to a building completed in 1980.

Another very English building is the Cathedral of St Michael and St George in Grahamstown, rebuilt by Gilbert Scott after 1860 but not completed until 1912. The result is a sober example of the Early English style, with a tower and spire. It is very different in character from a rather more enjoyable essay in Gothic of the type of which Scott and the ecclesiologists in England disapproved. This is the Roman Catholic Cathedral of Our Lady of the Flight to Egypt, Cape Town, begun in 1840 to the designs of a German architect called Sparman. The result is a building in very incorrect Gothic, whose meanness is redeemed by height and by the painted decoration of the interior. Externally, with its battlements, simplified detail and stuccoed walls, it looks more like a Gothic Revival church in India, where 'correctness' had to be qualified by the climate.

The most interesting as well as the most prominent Gothic Revival church in British India is a charming essay in the sort of Gothic current before the ecclesiologists laid down their rules in the 1840s. This is St Paul's Cathedral, Calcutta. The diocese was created in 1814 and the first proposal to build a new cathedral was made in 1819, but nothing was achieved until the time of Bishop Daniel Wilson. In 1839 the Bishop, who was a great church builder, appealed for money 'to erect a lofty and spacious airy church, in the Gothic, or rather Christian style of architecture, unencumbered by galleries; with an ample chancel or choir; and capable of seating about 800 or 1,000 persons'. This description might seem to be of a Gothic Revival church of the utmost rectitude, but the result, completed in 1846 and designed by Colonel W.N. Forbes of the Bengal Engineers, the architect of the Greek Revival Calcutta Mint, is not at all 'correct'. Beresford Hope, writing in 1861, could hardly contain his contempt: 'Almost with reluctance am I bound to note that the architecture of Calcutta Cathedral, the work of a colonel of engineers, can only be described as a sort of corrupt Perpendicular, apparently founded on some rude print of the Duomo of Milan. The steeple, to be sure, which seems successful, is modelled on

that of Norwich; the ceiling, it is scarcely necessary to say, is in no way amenable to any law of taste; while the internal arrangements, which allot the choir of a cathedral to the general congregation, can only be referred to as an example of what is to be avoided.'

In fact, the interior of the cathedral is very sensible in view of the climate and local traditions. There are no intervening columns, and the wide auditorium is covered by an elegant coved ceiling. Writing in her diary in 1884, the new Vicereine, Lady Dufferin, thought the cathedral 'rather like a railway station, the punkah rods representing the iron framework of that sort of building; the walls quite white, while the windows are a bluish colour, which makes everyone look pale. In deference to the hot climate the service was short.' The cathedral is altogether an unassuming design of great charm, especially with its outside walls faced in *chunam* and washed in colour. Following an earthquake, the Norwich steeple was replaced between 1934 and 1938 by a new one modelled on the Bell Harry tower at Canterbury.

Owing, no doubt, to the fact that military engineers continued to be responsible for the majority of buildings in India, this sort of pre-ecclesiological Gothic survived in church architecture. Christ Church, Simla, of 1857, and St George's, Hyderabad, of between 1865 and 1867, are both good examples of the style; both are evocative, unpretentious Gothic designs with battlements and single west towers; both are stuccoed. Interestingly, the contemporary Anglican church in Secunderabad, built for the British soldiers in the Hyderabad cantonments, is Classical in style. But the high seriousness of the Gothic Revival soon reached the presidency cities. The first example of 'correct' Gothic is St John's, or the Afghan Memorial Church, at Colaba, Bombay, designed in 1847 but not built until 1858. Anthony Salvin, J.M. Derick, and even Gilbert Scott might well have helped with the design. Scott himself sent out plans for the Church of St James on the Circular Road in Calcutta, built between 1861 and 1864.

With Gothic Revival public buildings going up in Bombay, it was inevitable that something should be done

St George's, Hyderabad, c 1865–7: an evocative
and unpretentious Gothic design.

about the poor, unpretentious old cathedral there. In 1865, James Trubshawe, Architect to the Ramparts Removal Committee in Bombay, and the designer of the new Post and Telegraph Offices, prepared plans for recasting the cathedral in a Gothic style into which he incorporated 'a sufficiency of Eastern features and traditions, to make it seem at home in a tropical climate, with ample characteristics of the Faith and the people it represents'. The building was to be given a new tower with a tall spire, but only a new apsidal and vaulted chancel had been added before the slump in the Bombay economy in the late 1860s brought work to a halt – and the obtrusive, high-pitched roof of Trubshawe's chancel has since been lowered.

Two impressive Gothic cathedrals built in India in the middle of Victoria's reign show some attempt to come to terms with the climate. All Saints' Cathedral, Allahabad, is remarkable as the work of a trained architect who actually knew India. William Emerson had been a pupil of William Burges, and had gone out to Bombay bearing the drawings of Burges' abortive project for the School of Art. Emerson stayed, and designed the Crawford Markets in Bombay and a church at Girgaum. Later, he designed Muir College in Allahabad and, finally, the Victoria Memorial in Calcutta. Allahabad Cathedral was begun in 1871 and completed in 1887. The design was 'semi-speluncar' in French Gothic with thick walls and the lower windows in the apse filled with stone *jalis* (pierced stone screens); it suggests, perhaps, what Burges might have achieved in Brisbane.

John Oldrid Scott provided an impressive and sensible design for Lahore Cathedral in 1880. The building is of cathedral proportions, vaulted throughout, and designed on the 'speluncar' principle with small windows, so that the interior is immensely dark and comparatively cool. The construction is of brick. Work began in 1883, and the twin west towers were completed in 1914 to a modified design. These have since been shorn of their saddleback tops owing to the danger of subsidence.

Holy Trinity Cathedral in Rangoon, Burma, is of interest as it was designed by Robert Chisholm of Madras, an architect who began by adapting Gothic to Indian conditions and who ended by employing the Indo-Saracenic style. In Rangoon, Chisholm used Gothic, but with the windows so arranged that no direct rays from the sun could enter the building. Work began in 1886, but economies caused the result to look rather different, when it was completed in 1894, from Chisholm's original design.

In the British colonies in Africa outside the Cape, a less archaeological type of Gothic, adapted to local conditions, was often employed. The most extraordinary example is Christ Church Cathedral, Lagos, Nigeria, which was rebuilt in concrete blocks between 1924 and 1935 in a charming and curiously naïve Gothic which looks as if it dates from a century earlier. As Basil Clarke observed, it 'was designed by an African architect, Mr J. Bagan Benjamin, in a Gothic style that it would be unfair to criticise from the point of view of those who demand strict correctness'.

Elsewhere in Africa, in the first few decades of the twentieth century, cathedrals and churches were being built from sophisticated designs sent out by distinguished British architects. Holy Trinity Church, Accra, was built in 1893 from designs prepared by Aston Webb, subsequently architect of the Victoria and Albert Museum in London, and the new front of Buckingham Palace. This church is the subject of that familiar legend that the wrong set of plans was sent out, and that the design intended for Africa was erected in some distant cold climate; but in the absence of precise information about where this might be, the joke is much diminished. Certainly the church in Accra, thirteenth-century Gothic in style, is completely English in character.

All Saints' Cathedral in Nairobi was designed in 1915 by Temple Moore, the architect of many austerely beautiful churches in England. The parts completed to his design – the nave, and two transepts with towers – are typical of his work, but accommodation was made to local conditions by the small size of the windows. St Paul's Cathedral, Kampala, Uganda, was designed by A. Beresford Pite after the previous building of brick and thatch had been struck by lightning. Beresford Pite was always an interesting, if not eccentric architect. In Brixton Road, London, he designed a

*All Saints' Cathedral, Nairobi, designed by Temple Moore
in 1915. The windows were reduced in size and other
modifications made later to suit the local climate.*

An isolated church on the Nakuru-Naivasha Road, Kenya.
If not architecturally outstanding, it is representative
of the long arm of imperial Christianity.

church in the Byzantine style; in Uganda he proposed a very simple, sensible Gothic building of brick with granite piers, roofs of local teak, and a central dome over a cruciform plan. It was consecrated in 1919.

All Saints' Cathedral in Khartoum was built between 1906 and 1913. It had been decided to build a cathedral there in 1900, partly as a memorial to General Gordon, two years after Omdurman and the reconquest of the Sudan. It was designed by Robert Weir Schultz (who subsequently changed his name to R.W.S. Weir), another architect who, like Beresford Pite, was influenced by Arts and Crafts ideals, and who was interested in Byzantine architecture. Khartoum Cathedral is more typical of this last, less imperialist, phase of ecclesiastical architecture in the British Empire, for Schultz twice visited the Sudan and carefully designed a church that reflected the local conditions and climate. The result is not a building that would look at home in England – although it should be said that Arts and Crafts architects such as Schultz and E.S. Prior did design churches in Britain with a self-conscious ruggedness and primitiveness.

The cathedral was built by local labour, under the direction of an experienced Scottish clerk of works. The primitive character of the design was appropriate to the traditional masonry construction. The sandstone was local: yellow and pale red. As timber was scarce, vaults were constructed without centring with rough bricks. To achieve insulation, the walls were thick, the windows small, and the roof double, with a sealed air-space between the vaults and an outer roof of pre-cast concrete slabs. The wooden furniture was made in England at Ernest Gimson's workshops at Sapperton. The arches of the interior are pointed in section and therefore Gothic in character, but there are hints in the geometrical piercing of the windows of Coptic and Egyptian Saracenic architecture, which Schultz had had the opportunity to study when he visited the Sudan in

1907. He travelled to Khartoum a second time for the consecration of the cathedral in 1912. A conspicuous feature of the design is the triangular window heads, made simply of two stone lintels which sometimes project proud of the wall surface to create shadow. When such shapes were used by Arts and Crafts architects in England they seem Anglo-Saxon in inspiration; in the Sudan they seem Arab in character. The sophisticatedly rugged detached tower was built later and completed in 1931. As a piece of architecture, Khartoum Cathedral is one of the best and most intelligent buildings in the British Empire; it is sad that, at present, it is quite inaccessible to visitors.

Even worse, Cairo Cathedral has been demolished. It was a fine building, decidedly twentieth-century in style, and yet appropriate to Egypt. All Saints' English Church had been built between 1873 and 1876 on a site donated by the Khedive Ismail. Rebuilding was proposed in 1915, and in 1916 Adrian Gilbert Scott, then serving in the Royal Engineers in Egypt, having been at Gallipoli, was invited to prepare designs. The first scheme, prepared in 1918, showed the influence of Adrian's elder brother Giles, and was in the Byzantine manner of Westminster Cathedral. Several further designs were made for different sites until a site by the Nile was bought in 1928. Owing to further difficulties with the foundations, construction did not begin until 1936, and the cathedral consecrated in 1938 was an entirely different design. The construction was of reinforced concrete, and the style a sort of stripped Romanesque, typical of church design at the time. Thick, solid walls were designed to reduce the heat and the few windows rose from floor level. At the west end stood a rather modernistic tower.

At the other end of Africa, one architect dominated church architecture in the early twentieth century, and this was a sophisticated designer anxious to respond to local conditions. Herbert Baker, who had gone to the Cape in

OPPOSITE *The Protestant Cathedral, Mombasa, Kenya, c1905: one of the first churches to break with the English mould and use vernacular architectural idioms.*

1892, was anxious to apply Arts and Crafts ideals in South Africa, and revive a traditional vernacular architecture. This was Cape Dutch. But in the area of ecclesiastical architecture, Baker did not have to persuade clients not to use imported, modern, prefabricated materials, as properly built Gothic had been established for churches by Sophie Gray. Baker's churches are, therefore, essentially in the Gothic Revival tradition, but given a ruggedness by the use of simple local materials: timber, brick and stone. This did not stop his designs from being over-ambitious, however; many of them incorporated tall, detached towers which were never built. The typical Baker church has walls of

Salisbury (Harare) Cathedral, designed by Herbert Baker and started in 1913.
Baker based his plan on the design of Pretoria Cathedral. He intended
that a round tower, influenced by the buildings of ancient Zimbabwe,
should form part of the building, but it was never executed.

Parish church at Port Maria, Jamaica, built in 1861.

squared rubble stone, inside as well as out. Often they are given apses, with windows placed high between rather mannered buttresses – which gives the buildings a definite turn-of-the-century character. Most are Gothic, but St Philip's, 'District Six', Cape Town, of 1898, is Romanesque, in brick and roughcast; St Mary's, Greyville, Durban, begun in 1912, is in a similar manner with an Italianate campanile added by Baker's partner, F.L.H. Fleming, and several of his designs have Gothic windows combined with internal round arches.

Baker's small parish churches, such as the Church of Christ, Arcadia, Pretoria, of 1906, and St George's, Parktown, Johannesburg, of 1904, seem much more sympathetic than his large cathedral projects. In Cape Town, it seems unforgivable that the old Greek Revival St George's, whose portico beautifully closed the vista up St George's Street, should have been replaced by Baker's un-metropolitan essay in Arts and Crafts Gothic. Baker's part of Pretoria Cathedral, the choir, built between 1905 and 1909 in a rugged, semi-Byzantine style, is a more impressive performance – different in character from the monumental Classic Union

Buildings which would rise nearby between 1910 and 1912. Baker used the style of Pretoria Cathedral for Salisbury (now Harare) Cathedral in Rhodesia (now Zimbabwe), built between 1913 and 1938. Here he also designed a circular tower, influenced by the buildings of ancient Zimbabwe, but this remains unexecuted.

Elsewhere in the world, Leonard Stokes, architect of Roman Catholic churches and telephone exchanges in England, designed the Roman Catholic Cathedral in Georgetown, British Guiana, begun in 1914; Adrian Gilbert Scott designed St James's Church in Vancouver in the 1930s; In Australia, St Andrew's Presbyterian Church in Brisbane, designed by G.D. Payne in 1910, is a good example of eclectic Arts and Crafts architecture, with imaginative detailing combining Romanesque with art nouveau. But the most interesting architect working in Australia in these years was John Cyril Hawkes, who was steeped in Arts and Crafts ideals. He had trained in England under Lethaby and J.D. Sedding, and, in 1909, had designed an Anglican church in the Bahamas. In 1912 he became a monk and took the name of Father Jerome. In

1915 the Franciscans sent him to Western Australia as a missionary and there he designed cathedrals, churches, convents, and presbyteries, in a strange, imaginative and eclectic Romanesque style. Perhaps his best buildings are St Francis Xavier's Cathedral and the Church of St Lawrence at Geraldton, and the Church of Our Lady of Mount Carmel and St Peter and St Paul at Mullewa. In 1940 Hawkes returned to the Bahamas. His career is reminiscent of that of Dom Paul Bellot, the French Benedictine architect-monk who designed the extraordinary Quarr Abbey on the Isle of Wight, and then went to Quebec where he designed a number of remarkable churches.

Last, but by no means least, there are the twentieth-century churches built in British India. Although he prepared designs, Lutyens did not build a cathedral church in New Delhi. In the event, the task of building churches fell to the younger architects who were Lutyens' and Baker's permanent representatives there, entrusted with supervising the construction of the new imperial capital. In 1925, H.A.N. Medd, Baker's assistant who had earlier worked for Lutyens, won the competition for the Anglican church. This, now the Cathedral Church of the Redemption, was built between 1927 and 1935 in a larger form on a different site. The result is a fine domed Classical church, well massed, which pays homage to Palladio's Il Redentore in Venice as well as to Lutyens. The interior, kept cool by massive walls and small windows, seems much more Anglican than Indian as it is an essay in the manner of Wren. Medd also won the competition for the Roman Catholic church. This too is now a cathedral, built between 1930 and 1934, and is a more streamlined design in brick, with strong horizontals and simple massing. Inside, Medd played with Classical arches of different sizes in the Lutyens manner.

In the military cantonments to the west of Delhi is St Martin's Garrison Church. This, designed by Lutyens' assistant, A.G. Shoosmith, and built of three-and-a-half million red bricks between 1928 and 1930, is not only one of the most brilliant examples of British colonial architecture, but also one of the finest buildings of the twentieth century. Shoosmith designed a building which seems modern in its austerity, and which is yet resonant with the power of the monuments of the ancient world. The sheer brick walls are stepped back alternately on each axis, as the building rises in the Lutyens manner, to create an almost brutal, yet subtly modelled, abstract mass. Penelope Chetwode recalls that when it was finished the English in Delhi called St Martin's the 'Cubist church'. The tower at the west end has no literal Gothic detail, yet by the careful recession of wall surfaces, the shape of buttresses and the character of a parish church steeple are suggested. The heat and dust of India were conquered by the few small and exquisitely placed windows in the massive walls – and the military liked this feature of the design as it suggested that the building could be defended in time of trouble. Inside, the church is plastered and is an austere, cool essay in the Lutyens Classical style.

St Thomas's, New Delhi, a brick church by Walter George, is another attempt at the style Shoosmith created for St Martin's. Such buildings may face difficulties in modern India, but, although British in character, they do not seem essentially out of place. Some colonial buildings erected in the lands that were once painted red on the map seem redundant and anachronistic in the independent Commonwealth or republican states which have succeeded the Empire. But cathedrals, churches and chapels on the whole do not. They are still needed, still used, and still maintained by local Christian congregations. After all, there are millions of Anglicans – let alone Roman Catholics and members of other denominations – in the world today, and only a small proportion are in Britain itself.

OPPOSITE *The Cathedral Church of the Redemption, New Delhi, designed by Henry Medd in 1928.*

Conclusion
Robert Fermor-Hesketh

BRITISH IMPERIAL ARCHITECTURE is usually conspicuous and almost always easy to identify. Yet too often criticism and praise have been confined to simple comparisons with contemporary buildings in England without any attempt being made to relate them to each other, or to fit them into a wider picture of which the architecture of the British Isles is only a part. Even the most grudging should admit that at the very least these buildings add great depth and perspective to the master models at home; at most, that many are genuinely original and worthy of considerable further study in their own right. Recognition of this fact is, unfortunately, only the first step towards a full appreciation of the value of colonial architecture, one problem being that the obvious connection between these buildings is the motivation of their architects rather than the nature of their style. The hopes, fears and ambitions of their builders were not merely the simple dreams of the traditional imperialists but the connecting links between a common body of architecture, spanning more than sixty modern countries.

A brief glance at the major colonial cities of the Empire reveals a remarkable level of continuity. Even if the British Empire has ceased to exist, an understanding of the nature of power has not; and while a few of the countries that were once part of it have completely abandoned the old buildings of British government and power, most have retained them without apparent change of purpose.

The houses of the Governor-Generals of Khartoum, New Delhi, Salisbury, Singapore, have become presidential palaces, and the better houses of the civil lines are still allocated to government servants according to grade. Military installations, particularly in India and Pakistan, seem to have remained untouched by time and change: the whitewashed stones shimmer still in the midday heat, and the long, low buildings stretch into the distance. The sheer volume of what remains, and its continued use, merits a different, and deeper, assessment of its historical and artistic worth.

Whether the imperial buildings have been retained or deliberately ignored says much about what has gone before, and something about the present and the future. What is certain is that these buildings are first-hand historical documents kept in a file which, in many cases, is still not closed.

A country's architecture is a near-perfect record of its history. Every building captures in a physical form the climate and resources of a country's geography; the social, economic, technological, and political conditions of its society; and the moral, philosophical, aesthetic, and spiritual values of its people.
(J.M. Freeland, *The Architecture of Australia*)

A unity of common interests can still be seen in the buildings that the Empire left behind. Their architectural styles varied, drawing sometimes on local culture for forms and decorative motifs, but more often on the European (though not always English) taste of the period. From a purist's point of view, their quirky identity does not add up to a unified architectural style, but rather to a rag-bag of styles imported from the other side of the world – usually in arrears of fashion. It is the architecture of the layman rather than the professional. The taste and ideals of the layman were always in evidence, even if they had been formed by the professional. British colonial architecture is the architecture of the familiar, re-created by an imperfect memory; and while it may not appeal to the classicist, it possesses an original personality of its own.

Its governing influences were often far more basic than is generally realized: fashion did play a part, but with varied effects within different groups. There is a fundamental difference between the desire to re-create a little corner of England in a foreign field, on the one hand, and the desire to produce buildings which challenged the British originals in style and opulence, on the other. Melbourne and Vancouver were stating their future independence for anyone who cared to listen. There is no nostalgia for Britain there, as is to be found in much of the colonial domestic architecture of India. The distinction is an important one because it highlights two entirely different colonial groups: the adminstrators and the settlers. The administrator, often born in the colonies, was usually sent back to England for his education, and was cocooned on his return by a rigid, British society. His life was bound by limits, and his own abilities by the certainties of promotion and eventual pension. Retirement to some kind of gentility was inevitable. Neither the hill station of his creation, nor its architecture, is to be found in settlers' colonies. The half-timbered houses of Nuwara Eliya, Ceylon, Fraser's Hill, Malaysia, and Darjeeling, in north-eastern India, are the eastern equivalent of Sunningdale, and are entirely escapist in concept and execution. Travellers' frequently cited comparisons with Wales and Scotland are all part of a pattern of conscious self-delusion. Thomas Babington Macaulay described the approaches to Ootacamund in the Nilgiri hills as having 'the vegetation of Windsor Forest or Blenheim spread over the hills of Cumberland'. Lord Lytton, Viceroy of India from 1876 to 1880 was to write in a similar vein: 'Imagine Hertfordshire

Detail from the wall decoration in a public lavatory, Durban, South Africa.

Prince of Wales Hotel, Niagara on the Lake, Ontario : the principal hotel in one of the best preserved nineteenth-century towns in North America.

Bellevue House, Kingston, Ontario, built in 1840. It was once the home of Canada's first Prime Minister, John Macdonald.

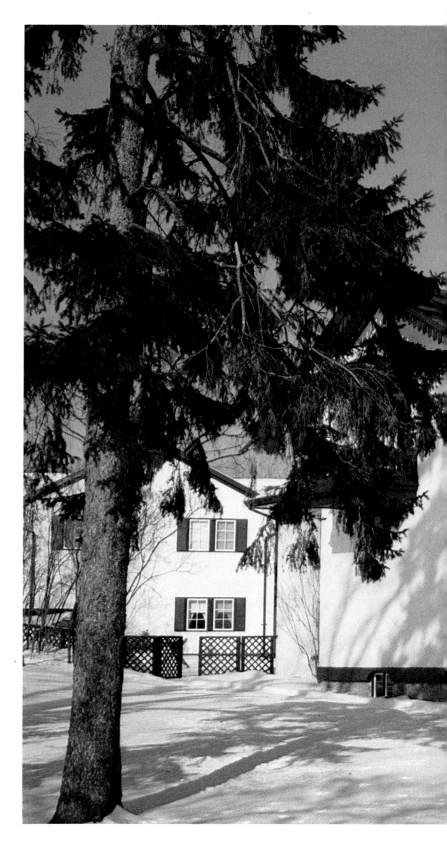

Naini Tal Hill Station, c 1900.

lanes, Devonshire downs, Scotch trout streams … Such beautiful English rain, such delicious English mud.' The hill stations contain nothing of India, Ceylon (Sri Lanka) or Malaya. They were as much an escape from the country itself as from the heat and humidity of the plains. They enshrine the architecture of exiles – a self-indulgence which allowed the rigidly maintained façade to slip, away from prying eyes.

The details of this illusion are fascinating. The interiors of the houses excluded all local artefacts. The gardens had English lawns, English blooms and English privet hedges. The towns contained English-style theatres – Simla had the 'Gaiety' – teashops, a public library, and a promenade, usually called the Mall. This carefully maintained illusion proved to be the nearest that many men ever came to a Western ideal of a balanced society. Climate, frequent postings and low pay all militated against early marriage, and the many who craved normality were intent on making it a British normality. The vast number of servants might have marred the true Britishness of this picture for the critical observer, but they were after all considered to be invisible – an attitude of mind that came more naturally with practice.

The administrators' brand of colonial architecture was quite alien to the settlers' colonies – as were the principles it stood for. This was partly because they were expatriates by choice, but, more fundamentally, because the settlers were consciously building something of their own, and their reality lay within themselves. European administrators often scattered far more widely than the settlers, and the annual summer retreat acquired a psychological significance that is not readily understandable today. Modern communications make it extremely difficult to imagine the self-imposed isolation that was the lot of so many imperial servants.

The first, and, as a general rule, the majority of colonies were founded for reasons of trade rather than state. Restrictions imposed on personal freedom and conscience were a frequent cause for emigration, but the success of an overseas colony depended on trade to supply its basic needs, and on marketable resources to pay for them. Increasing control from the centralized imperial secretariat invariably followed, most often caused by local upheavals which required a military solution beyond the means of the merchant community. A planned imperial design was very much a creation of the nineteenth century, when the Empire was beginning to decline.

None of the early outposts of the Empire was a 'balanced' community, and a trained architect was very low on the list of priorities. The earliest buildings therefore reflected styles and techniques familiar to their creators, not so much from a lack of imagination as from the desire to achieve the simplest solution to a not very important problem.

Time changed this attitude, and the age of a colony is usually reflected in the extent to which local decorative motifs have been absorbed with the evolution of architectural styles imported from the home country. The hybrid results of gradual assimilation often have a homeless look to them, but some, such as the buildings of imperial New Delhi, would look out of place in any setting other than their own.

The self-assurance of these buildings, in the middle of the north Indian plain, lies in the Indian understanding of empire, an understanding far older than the British presence. In a country with eight hundred million inhabitants, and over a hundred languages, these, the last and most imposing of British imperial buildings, are still in a sense the buildings of an imperial capital. Even so, while they may look Indian to an Englishman, they do not to an Indian.

The Victoria Memorial Hall in Madras, while less well known, provides a better example. It is pure imperial Indo-Saracenic in style, and apart from the basic concept of a memorial hall – itself quintessentially English – stylistically it owes nothing to English architecture. Its proportions, however, are European – and it is this factor which gives many imperial buildings an alien aspect as far as the indigenous races are concerned. European proportions and use of space almost always give away the origins of a colonial building, particularly so in domestic architecture. Often it appears unfamiliar at first glance, but is perfectly logical

*Victoria Memorial Hall, Madras. Designed by Henry Irwin and built
in 1909, it was modelled on the main gateway at
Fatehpur Sikri, and now houses the National Art Gallery.*

when examined more closely. The differences lie in a practical adaptation to circumstance rather than to architectural competence. Much of the space in an English country house was occupied by servants and rooms necessary to their various functions. These were confined to the attics and basement, and, in some cases, to the wings. Hot climates made attics unusable, and also obviated the need for extensive storage space for food. Food went off so quickly

that, in the interests of health, there could be no question of maintaining comprehensive larders. Servants who would normally have occupied considerable living space did not do so. Most servants in the colonies were native family men and women who lived with their families in separate compounds. Their religious beliefs, particularly in relation to food and its preparation, made this imperative rather than merely a social convenience. Religious prohibitions, particulary in India, ran very deep and were not negotiable. For this very reason, Europeans in India employed what can seem to be an excessive number of servants until it is remembered that caste prevented most Hindus from doing more than one narrowly defined job. The combination of these factors drastically reduced the need for specialized space, and thus redefined its use.

This redefining of space could take the form of a simple raising of the height of the ceilings, which did not alter the outward aspect of the house, and had the huge advantage of vastly improving the flow of air through the living spaces. High ceilings and large central halls were to be found in many of the great houses of the Caribbean sugar islands and the southern states of America. The solution to the problem of heat, first adopted in India and later evolved in Australia, was the low-roofed bungalow. Where it was not adopted, as at Government House, Parramatta, New South Wales, the heat in the upper storey during the hot months became almost intolerable.

The bungalow was to become the imperial domestic dwelling. Its origins lay in India, but its adaptability and convenience were to take the basic idea to the ends of the earth. Whether it was a simple mud building on the burning plains or an elaborate wooden structure on stilts, as it was to become in Queensland and Malaya, the bungalow was home.

The Australians were to bring the basic bungalow design to its highest peak, both aesthetically and practically. It has

A typical Australian bungalow, the sort of house in which the vast majority of people lived, though such buildings are rarely given the attention they deserve.

Bungalow at Maryborough, Queensland. This style, developed at the end
of the nineteenth century, was created specifically to meet
local needs, and is arguably Australia's only indigenous architecture.

been suggested that its initial appearance in Australia was the result of a misconception. Bungalows had arrived in England from India by the end of the eighteenth century, and the suggestion is that the design was taken to Australia by an Englishman living in England rather than by an old hand in the colonial Indian administration. The rapid adaptation of the basic design would suggest that its full benefits were not initially understood. Early Australian bungalows were one room wide, with a verandah at the front which provided an outside passage to connect the rooms. However, Experiment Farm, Parramatta, and Claremont Cottage, Windsor, both built in the early 1820s, show evidence of far more sophisticated thinking in their designs. The overall plans are elegant, and the verandahs are incorporated into the structure rather than being a mere addition. An evolution in design had taken place with the same kind of strong connection with the prototype that Anglo-Palladianism has with the Palladian originals. Certainly, with the incorporation of the low roof line into the main structure, the change from a long, rectangular ground-plan to a much squarer and deeper one, and the extension of the verandah round three, and sometimes all four, sides of the house, the Australian bungalow achieved a level of architectural sophistication never seen in India.

The design was at once practical and cool, providing a neat solution to the perennial problem of low-quality building materials which had plagued early Australian structures. The verandah simply carried the rainwater beyond the line of the walls, thus greatly reducing any damage to the bricks and mortar. If high architectural theory were missing, pragmatism and good taste triumphed where other virtues might not.

This process of adaptation did not apply to religious architecture, which, of all forms of colonial building, adhered most closely to English taste. The mosque-like Protestant cathedral in Mombasa is an exception – but a late exception. Churches were an exact reflection of contemporary English architectural taste, and were, in many cases, designed by English architects.

If religious architecture is the most intransigent and inflexible aspect of the Empire, it is worth remembering that the modern lack of a strong and coherent spiritual life would have been completely incomprehensible in colonial times. Imperial subjects of the nineteenth century instinctively understood formal religion, and indeed practised it as their descendants do today.

Though the nature of colonial Christianity is outside the scope of this book, its effect cannot be completely ignored. For the Englishman, Christianity provided a familiarity and certainty that was an immensely important part of his self-confidence. A short walk round the Park Street Cemetery in Calcutta, or that of any colonial cantonment, is enough to indicate that if he understood little else the colonial Englishman understood his own mortality. The strength derived from religion, and the role it still plays in many African and Caribbean countries, is one of the longer-lasting

imperial legacies. Christianity was for the Briton one of the few certainties in an uncertain world. Change and innovation were part of his everyday life, and the Church provided a star of constancy to steer by.

Colonial insecurities were very real, and could hardly fail to affect architectural development. The modern vision of the invincible British Empire is for the most part accurate, but applies only to the middle of the nineteenth century. At the end of the eighteenth century, the British population in the colonies was minuscule. Architectural development, like imperial power, came later than is usually realized.

Ignorance and inertia were as common then as they are now, but the architecture of the early colonists owed as much to their deeper psychological needs as it did to either of these failings.

St Nicholas' Plantation House in Barbados is an exact copy of a west country manor. It had been commissioned by a man who had never previously been to the Caribbean, but who had enough money to ensure the comforts of home. The commission included a drawing room with two fireplaces, which showed a rather greater feeling for Dorset than for Barbados. In the days before air travel and rapid communication, most people were – naturally – extremely ignorant of any country other than their own; almost all contemporary travel books and memoirs show an elastic regard for the truth, and concentrate on the aggrandisement of the author and his exploits. In consequence, early domestic colonial dwellings are often not only very uncomfortable but also display vividly the workings of last-minute empirical improvisation.

Sheer size too can often soothe insecurities, and this was the solution which was chosen in Calcutta. The city needed an impressive Government House, and, in the absence of a trusted professional architect, an English country house was selected and reproduced on a scale thought suitable to the occasion. Thus it was that Kedleston Hall, in Derbyshire, was imitated, on twice the scale, in the middle of Calcutta. The transposed detail of the elevation, interior and decoration included copies even of the statuary – though with their bosoms removed at the last minute in case they

*Gerraghty's store in Maryborough, Queensland: one of
the few survivors of an endangered species.*

offended Lord Wellesley. The scale was indeed imposing, and probably did as much to reassure the Europeans as to overawe the Indians. It would in fact have been seen by only a minute percentage of the Indian population of Bengal, as travel was extremely difficult even for the small number who had the means.

In settlers' colonies architectural evolution was practical. Trained craftsmen were hard to come by, and it took time to build up a body of skilled workmen. Many were largely self-taught, their experience linked to local materials and climatic conditions rather than to the more sophisticated trade practices of contemporary England. This was most marked in Australia, where convicts were selected for their different skills when sent for deportation.

The roof of the Rum Hospital in Sydney typifies the flaws and benefits of this practice. It was built with a simple extension of the 'open couple system' that was used on the earliest huts, the ceiling joists being set across the building independently of the rafters. Short timber lengths (the only ones available) also necessitated the use of short spans which, in any case, were all that the outer walls could stand. Technically the system was totally unsuited to a building of any size, being structurally unsound, but it did produce the combination of pleasing proportions and light roof lines so typical of early Australian buildings. The significance of this is open to two interpretations: 'crude copies' is a common, if uncharitable, description of Australian Georgian architecture; there seems to be a much stronger case for seeing it as

*Bungalow, Maryborough, Queensland. Raising the
living quarters on stilts protected
the inhabitants from termites and permitted a vast variety of
decorative detail.*

ABOVE *Lord Nelson Hotel, Sydney, 1843. This is
the last surviving corner-site hotel in Sydney
dating from the mid-nineteenth century.*

part of a genuine evolution, containing truly original elements and providing, at the very least, footnotes without which any thorough assessment of the original models is incomplete.

The abundance, rather than the shortage, of materials was to be significant in the American colonies. Buildings in Britain were using more and more brick and stone as wood became scarcer and more expensive, but in America wood of good quality and suitable size was readily available, and a large pool of craftsmen existed. Many of the first arrivals in America were highly skilled, and were faced with an unfamiliar wealth of an entirely familiar material. They were involved in private enterprise rather than a public one, and the early colonists seem to have had a far greater grasp of the practical details of the problems posed by an alien territory than was shown at Botany Bay a century and a half later.

It comes as no surprise that in America the first colonial buildings were thoroughly English in aspect, since their builders were themselves English. The origins of many of the earliest buildings in New England can be traced directly, by the distinctive work of the carpenters, to the medieval villages from which the settlers originated, many in East Anglia.

Large numbers of timber-framed buildings in America are still constructed along the lines of the basic designs of the earliest ones. Thomas Jefferson was to complain of 'the unhappy prejudice ... that houses of brick and stone [were] less wholesome than those of wood'. It was a prejudice that affected all classes, and, as late as the mid-nineteenth century, Texan plantations still shipped wood from Galveston for the building of houses, while attractive local limestone was generally used for outbuildings and slave quarters. Availability and cost, then as now, were two of the greatest attractions of wood.

The American War of Independence came at a rather inconvenient moment from the point of view of the architectural historian, because it was in this decade that the American colonies were to witness the beginning of an architectural movement of real originality and style. It says a great deal about American, and nothing pleasant about British, perspicacity that the American colonies had developed an independence of intellectual thought which was, in architectural terms, exemplified by Thomas Jefferson at Monticello. The Neo-Classical Federalist buildings of the following decades were built in an independent country, but were intellectually conceived in the period of colonial America. It is not, however, for an English author to lay a post-dated claim to American cultural gems. But architectural development in America after 1776 does raise one very important question: in the light of the unavoidably close tie that a colony must have with its mother country, is it possible for its architecture totally to break away from the fashion prevailing at home? In the American experience, the best of the architects had, intellectually speaking, broken with England before 1776. The loyalists who went north to Canada took with them all the old designs, and sometimes the very houses, but none of the new ideas. The answer would, therefore, seem to be No. The architecture of a settlers' colony was closely linked to its political and cultural state of mind. The granting at an early date to Canada and Australia of the status of dominion, and the right to self-government, shows that this was better understood in the nineteenth century than it had been in 1776.

The British in South Africa were also to adopt local styles: in their case it was those of the Dutch, from whom they had captured the colony. The Dutch gable continued to be almost as prevalent after their departure as it had been during their tenure. French Canada is also, to this day, visibly more French in aspect than anything else. The

OPPOSITE Ground floor of a terrace house, Sydney.
The iron used in balconies and railings such as these
frequently came to Australia as ballast in the ships.

*An eighteenth-century private house, Philadelphia. Without being flamboyant
in any sense, this kind of house was representative
of the growing commercial wealth and strength of America.*

simple truth was that the British were quite prepared to use any building style that could be adapted to their living patterns. The pride of nation that does surface from time to time was usually, in architectural terms, subconscious rather than conscious, and the familiar was often the easiest and sometimes the only choice, rather than being merely a mirror of the insensitivity of the colonial power.

These considerations did not apply to the colonies in India and the Far East. There could be no question of a white independence, as the native population so far outnumbered the colonial power and its servants as to make this impossible. India, in particular, possessed a very highly developed culture of its own, and a distinguished architectural tradition. Whether or not this was properly appreciated (the ability to do so being most apparent in families who had lived in India for some time), it was a very strong force towards the development of architectural styles that was to take place at the turn of the century. Those families who had served for generations in the merchants' houses and the administration were often, quite naturally, more closely attuned to their surroundings. Too often the newcomers dismissed what they did not understand. Whether or not attempts to combine different cultures in a single architectural essay were successful should not obscure the value of the effort made.

One result of the British assimilation of ethnic architectural styles was the influence of Indo-Saracenic architecture on the Decorative Arts movement in England, particularly in the hands of Lockwood Kipling, the father of Rudyard. Earlier attempts at 'exotica' had been made in England, and included Sezincote and the Brighton Pavilion. In practice, this early blend of styles was applied more to decoration than to architecture.

A curious footnote to this process of assimilation is that authentic Indo-Saracenic buildings are sometimes referred to by the Indians – in modern Bombay, for example – as 'our' imperial buildings, and, standing as they do among towering apartment blocks, they have come to be admired. They are now regarded with an affection and respect similar to that accorded to Victorian architecture in

England over the last twenty years.

Two important considerations influencing all architecture – civil, military, or private – is the availability of both money and architects. The simplest and most obvious statement of pride in achievement in architectural terms is size; the houses of the great nineteenth-century magnates and rising industrialists in Great Britain bear witness to this. The Victorian age created a great deal of ready money, which was beginning to supersede the power based on landed wealth – and money, not land, builds houses. But the colonies frankly did not have the financial resources to build the kind of country houses which were so common in England, even if they had wished to do so. The fabled English nabobs of India preferred, in any case, to build at home upon their retirement. Colonial country houses are more closely tied to their owners' needs than to their self-image.

Government buildings suffered under the same restrictions, but often it was because the government refused to spend the money rather than because of an outright lack of it. Government House, Calcutta, was commissioned by Lord Wellesley without official permission, just as Lord Curzon, unauthorized, later commissioned the Viceregal Lodge at Simla, but this kind of *fait accompli* was something that few could get away with, and most Governors were faced with the same kind of expediencies as was Governor Macquarie in New South Wales. His request for an architect and money for a new hospital in Sydney was turned down by Lord Liverpool, back in London, who decided that Sydney did not need a new hospital, and that it needed an architect neither for this nor for any other project. The building was finally designed by Francis Greenway and paid for by granting a monopoly on 45,000 gallons of rum.

Despite the intrinsic wealth of the colonies, the Colonial Office operated on a restricted budget, while the imperial government strenuously avoided paying for anything if it could possibly help it. It is not surprising that this attitude is often reflected in its building projects. It should in fairness be said that money was more readily available for civil engineering projects, which were more likely to show a

Government House, Ganesh Khind, Poona. Designed by James Trubshawe, it was
built c1855 and its tall, slim tower (which contains the water tanks)
has been described as a 'Victorian rendering of an Italian campanile'.

profit, such as the Ganges irrigation canals.

Often as shadowy as the architects themselves are those who commissioned the buildings. The Empire had its share of stereotypes, but for every one there was an opposite: for every revolutionary in America, there was a loyalist; for every Briton who despised the Empire, there was an Indian who admired it; for every Boer on commando, there was one serving with the British Army; for every free settler in Australia, there was an ex-convict who was as rich. Even divisions by class are complex and elusive. The upper class and the working class are comparatively easy to identify: one provided the Governor-Generals and commissioned many of the buildings; the other, the private soldiers who did most of the work. Almost every other public office was administered by persons who belonged to neither class. The backbone of the Empire was the professional classes, in

*Viceregal Lodge, Simla, designed by Henry Irwin for the
Viceroy in 1888, very much in the style of the
Scottish hydro hotel. It owes nothing to its surroundings.*

charge of funds and public works departments. All too many men who had made decisions affecting millions retired to genteel poverty in Bath or Cheltenham, with little to offer their sons beyond contacts to advance their careers. Privilege existed, undoubtedly, but usually gave young men little more than a good education and sometimes a small private income. Those with large private incomes stayed at home. The imperium was never over-generous to its servants. It is these men who were largely responsible for the architectural stereotypes of the Empire. If their architecture was often middle of the road, so were they. The governmental bungalows and officers' quarters, allocated according to rank, are their legacy. The Queen Victoria Barracks in

Hong Kong, the barracks at the Red Fort, New Delhi, and those at Meerut, Rawalpindi and Parramatta are their work. For the most part, these were men educated to a sense of duty, service and Christianity: often ambitious, usually efficient, occasionally greedy and brutal, but very rarely corrupt, they formed a small percentage of imperial colonists and would be familiar today in the middle and upper grades of the Civil Service. Public Works Department buildings, often called by another name, are the same the world over – usually worthy, avoiding the flamboyant. Many of the larger buildings are better, but all give the same impression that the office is rather greater than the man. The domestic buildings were limited to a very small selection of designs which were comfortable if not very luxurious (though some would not agree), and interchangeable within the different territories of the Empire. No civil service has ever encouraged aesthetic considerations to take into account its employees' varying tastes.

Military architecture was affected by the same constraints of accountability, but is, nonetheless, often surprisingly attractive. It was far in advance of anything in England at that time, being high-roofed, airy, spacious, healthy and clean. The Victoria Barracks in Darlinghurst, Sydney, and the Lancer Barracks in Parramatta were as good as any in the world – and the former are still in use today, almost unchanged. The imperial fortifications are dull by comparison, but then the Empire never required anything to compare with the mathematical glories of Vauban or the Spanish fortresses of San Cristobal or El Moro in Puerto Rico. Controlling the sea, the Empire relied on manoeuvre and reinforcement rather than on vast, fixed fortifications which could be defended for months on end without assistance.

Numerous forts and fortifications are scattered all over the imperial domains, but they are all designed for limited action against a local enemy, not for full-scale defence against a European army. Almost all are unsophisticated in both the military and the architectural senses, and very few were intended to be garrisoned after they had served their purpose. Fortresses never served the British Empire as permanent symbols of domination. A colony in a state of perpetual insurrection was a steady financial drain, and all efforts were made to find a civil rather than a military solution. The lack of permanent fortifications was to cause a major embarrassment on several occasions, in particular at Ladysmith and Lucknow. The truth was, very simply, that the British, being an island race, were not great military engineers in the tradition of European nations who had to defend lengthy, land-locked borders.

Many an old soldier would still recognize the colonial parade grounds of his youth. Rawalpindi, Simonstown, Dum Dum, Meerut and Bangalore are all as military as ever: the uniforms, the traditions, the drills are all largely unchanged; some of the officers are still trained at Sandhurst; the men in the élite regiments are still as smart. The barracks and cantonments lie as near the heart of the Empire as any other group of buildings. They are found everywhere in the former colonies, and they too have changed little. Almost all these ex-colonies have armies founded on a level of excellence rather than on the principles of a 'people's army'. The entry of politics into many of these armies is not a British legacy, though much else is.

If the Empire is best remembered for occasional *folies de grandeur* rather than for its mighty forts, its worthiest architectural legacy is its Georgian buildings. Private and professional taste coincided and combined in a colonial Georgian style which is neither wholly derivative nor wholly imitative, but possesses some originality. The verandah, always a central feature in hot countries, was, for a brief time, an uneasy addition to an otherwise Classical plan. It was rapidly (and often very elegantly) incorporated into a well-thought-out design. Palladian and Georgian themes were often reduced to great simplicity, but it was far from being a mindless simplicity. If the amateur architects were untrained, they were neither ignorant nor uneducated; their buildings may often lack sophistication, but they are based on sound architectural principles.

Much colonial Georgian architecture had merits of its own. The great buildings of imperial power that were to rise along the streets of Ottawa, Delhi and Melbourne had little to do with the Georgian style, but examples of the idiom that have survived as in Spanish Town, Jamaica, are charming if small by comparison. Calcutta and Madras had a richer Georgian legacy, but the imperatives of commercial development were no less damaging then than today, and little of the period remains.

Though similar in appearance to an English country house, the colonial equivalent played a more serious role in society, which was in many ways a throwback to earlier times in England. They were often the centre for administration and justice, and provided rallying points in times of unrest. With greater centralized control by the government this role diminished, but the duality was still to apply to the

Governor-Generals' residences. They were often to combine the positions of the chancery and residence of a modern embassy, but with far greater powers. The Viceregal Lodge at Simla was, for the summer months, the centre of imperial bureaucracy in India, and it stood for a great deal more than just a long summer's holiday.

Colonial Georgian is currently the most admired of the many colonial styles, and it is based root and branch in the principles of Anglo-Palladianism. This was, arguably, England's answer to the architecture of Catholic Europe – and Baroque Catholic Europe in particular. It makes statements about prosperity, self-confidence and fundamental beliefs that transcend mere architectural detail. In that many of these beliefs have been accepted in their countries of adoption, where contact with the original source has become minimal, the architecture that enshrines them is more than mere bricks and mortar. In simple terms, these are the buildings of Government, Justice and the Church.

The true source of all colonial wealth and power was trade, and the social position of traders and merchants changed significantly as the Empire spread. In two hundred years, Hawkins, Drake and Raleigh had been transformed from every schoolboy's heroes into a collection of anachronisms. The new heroes of the Empire were the creations of Kipling, Henty and Rider Haggard. No less courageous and inventive, but with considerably less of the Elizabethans' brashness, they were public school, for Queen and Country. The later Empire was not represented in its ideology by the Clyde Bank engineers or the crews of the tea clippers or the workers in the Kalgoorlie gold fields and the diamond fields of Africa – and yet it was these men who produced the wealth of much of the Empire.

No single group had a greater impact in its time than the British traders but, sadly, their passage is often hard to recognize: many of their buildings were the first to be destroyed in the name of change, progress, and the

In the gardens of the Hyderabad Residency, commissioned by Major James Achilles Kirkpatrick, is this model of the building. Kirkpatrick married Khair-un-Nissa, the daughter of a noble family of Persian descent. She lived in strict purdah and never saw the main house (see opposite).

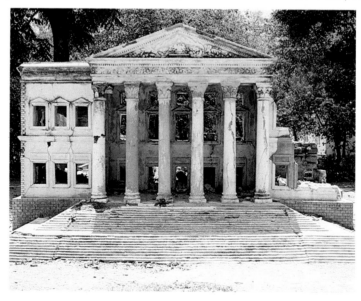

The Residency, Hyderabad, designed by Lieut. Samuel Russell
of the Madras engineers and begun in 1803.

economic necessity of hard cash in the shape of property speculation. The architecture of State and Church incorporated the principles of government, justice, defence, and much more – but more than anything, it typified the principles of permanence. If little else remains of gold towns like Hill End in New South Wales, the church and hospital are still there. Sometimes in Australia it is the court house which has survived, often it is the gaol, but always it is the buildings representative of a functioning State. Trade was the antithesis of permanence, relying as it did on constant change – or, more accurately, on constant adaptation to a world that had never before changed so fast. There are still a few relics – the ruined Stock Exchange at Ballarat, Victoria, the warehouses in Hobart and in Kuching, Sarawak – but the trading world looks to the future and not to the past. When the merchants built, they built whole cities where none had been before: think of Calcutta, Bombay, Singapore and Hong Kong. If their individual buildings remain, it is only because they still fulfil their purpose, or because they have, for some reason, been passed over by 'progress'. Symbols were for the civil service and the churches; theirs are practical buildings, not ones enshrining principles.

Sugar Mill, Wentworth Plantation, Jamaica, late eighteenth century: an unusually lavish design for a functional building of this kind.

*Higginbotham's, Madras: the principal book store, their services included the
provision of English comics for the Governor-General's children.*

Godown (or warehouse) in Mombasa, Kenya,
decorated like a Wedgwood plate.

Bandstand in Mombasa, Kenya.

Singapore and Hong Kong are the modern day success stories of the merchant city state. Their architecture is entirely mercantile in conception and creation, but their very success has destroyed the relics of earlier generations. Continuing progress and vitality have ensured the destruction of many of the great dockland vistas. While this may be a tragedy for the architectural historian, it does have a certain ironic justice. The architecture of a trading empire was its servant rather than its memorial.

Trade both affected and infected everything imperial. Despite the constant and bitter social sneers of the nineteenth and twentieth centuries, the imperial presence always followed regularized trading arrangements, a practice for which a specific architecture was introduced. The high-minded buildings of government achieved a prominence even now far beyond their due. The great civic buildings of Bombay, Ottawa, Melbourne or Singapore – the schools, universities, libraries, hospitals, banks and hotels – all represent the ever-increasing wealth, power and pride of the merchant community. If they demonstrate any kind of gut feeling, it is not that 'we are better than the Indians or the Chinese', but that 'we are better than Liverpool or Birmingham'.

This feeling is prevalent in the trading cities of India and the Far East, but it is just as true of the great cities of Australia, Canada and South Africa. The granting at a surprisingly early date of the status of dominion, and therefore of home rule, to the settlers' colonies was a reaction to the increasing self-confidence and independence of these states. Often the architecture is confused, but even if a strange copy of the Cloth Hall at Ypres creeps into view, it must be stressed that none of these cities is a simple transportation of a foreign city to another clime. Australia is the best example of this independent attitude of mind. Many emigrants had left England with little feeling of affection for their country of origin. Indeed, in the case of most of the ex-convicts, there was none, and the success of the colony and its increase in wealth had created a considerable local self-confidence. There was a strong feeling of achievement, despite interference from the government, which was partly due – regrettably – to the suppression of the Aborigines. This eliminated for the time being (though the problem was to resurface with a vengeance) most of the immediate racial difficulties which were to cause so many upheavals elsewhere.

This transformation from a dependency to a new and independent country is a process not readily understandable today, in a world where all land is accounted for, and, in most cases, vastly over-populated. The architecture of Australia, and some of the other settlers' colonies, was created by people who thought in terms of absolutes, and not in the infinite variations of a more complex modern world. Graziers, farmers, merchants, traders, even labourers, believed in their land of opportunities – and if their cities reflect naïve pride and spirit, it is theirs alone, and not something created by the Empire.

The later architecture of trade has even less stylistic coherence than that of the early nineteenth century. More often than not, it is a local variation of the 'Edwardian composite' – the offshoot of the eclectic 'Gothick Revival' at home. It is best expressed in the railway station at Kuala Lumpur, the Prince of Wales Museum in Bombay, the warehouses of Dacca or the Istana of Rajah Brook in Kuching.

Colonial governments and traders, administrators and settlers all – in the later years of the Empire – adopted architectural styles which were part of a generalized international trend and did not exclusively derive from Britain. Air conditioning came into use after the Second World War, and swiftly obviated the need for buildings to be adapted to the vagaries of the climate. Skyscrapers and Departments of Works, interchangeable, anonymous, wholly forgettable concrete blocks, won the day in the Empire – as they did elsewhere. Little is left except the buildings themselves: the later British Empire has had an embarrassingly small impact on the daily lives of the millions who were once its subjects.

The impact on a more profound level has, however, been enormous, and, for many nations, irreversible. Any final judgement on the architectural legacy of this Empire must be symbolic as well as aesthetic. Over sixty member states of the United Nations were once encompassed within the circle of the Empire, and the buildings that remain belong as much to them as they do to Britain. The British, despite their once insatiable territorial ambitions, have always been intensely insular in their cultural opinions. Colonial architecture can seem a very small part of the nations' cultural heritage, and in the sense that it was the work of a small number of people, and the product of a relatively short period of British history, this is an illusion easy to accept. However, to other nations many of these buildings have a considerable historical significance. It is rather like looking down the wrong end of a telescope. Over one billion people in these countries have never seen the architecture of England, and over ninety-nine per cent of the sixty-odd million in Britain have never visited a single nation that once belonged to the Empire. Rather more may have seen an old sepia photograph of a faded and obscure building, an antiquated figure in a rather strange hat standing stiffly in the foreground. A judgement must be made in purely aesthetic terms as to how competent or original these buildings were. Though one must admit that few of them

Euston, Hong Kong, built as a private house by Mr Eu.
The design reflects contemporary ambitions rather than any prevailing architectural style.
His other house, Euclyffe, which has been pulled down, was much uglier.

*Spencer's store, Madras. This was 'the' imperial store
in southern India, with branches in most important towns.*

were truly unique, it is in the qualifications to this that much that is best about colonial architecture lies.

There is something incontrovertibly different about them which is difficult to qualify, but which would make them seem very out of place in England. Drayton, in South Carolina, has a two-tier portico which was common in the south because of the weather, and rare in England for precisely the same reason. The Vassall-Longfellow house in Cambridge, Massachusetts, is conventional in appearance, but timber-framed in brightly painted wood. English houses tend to have central chimneys in order to heat the maximum number of rooms, whereas the southern plantation houses tended to have them at the end of the house in order that the cool air might pass through the house in the summer months. Use of materials, patterns, simplifications, and transposition of details, all contribute to this differentiation.

Great emphasis has been placed on the use of the pattern book as the sole source of inspiration, particularly in America, and some houses and churches were indeed little more than copies, but it should not be forgotten that this was true of England too. Some American houses were closely based on English ones. Shirley Place, in Massachusetts, was little more than a copy of Wilbury House, Wiltshire. The books provided designs, floor plans, and details for any aspiring architect to use in building a house to the latest taste, in the same way that the Anglo-Palladians had found their inspiration in Italy. They were used extensively in Great Britain as well as in the American colonies. By 1760, colonial records list over fifty such works published in England, the most influential being *Palladio Londinensus; or, The London Art of Building*. By no stretch of the imagination could this number have been published exclusively for the colonial market, which in any case considered itself, and was looked upon, as British. Some houses drew directly on Italy anyway – Stratford, in Virginia, was at least partly drawn from Sebastiano Serlio's *Architettura*. The Provost's House at Trinity College, Dublin, was built from an unpublished drawing by Palladio in the possession of Lord Burlington. Three variants were built in London, Potsdam, and Dublin, of which the latter is the sole survivor.

But from first to last much of the architecture of the British Empire was designed by British architects, and should be judged in that light. After all, Roman and Greek colonial architecture is not divided by an artificial barrier of origin; nor is it judged on the merits of their unwelcome rule, but solely on the merits of what has survived. A Roman court house in England, would, if such a thing existed, be an object of veneration owing to the principles it enshrined and its great antiquity. Its architectural merits would run a poor third, and its relevance as a symbol of Roman colonialism would hardly be considered. Neither would the absence of a named architect be held against it. Yet these criteria, particularly the latter, have consistently prevented the making of a balanced appraisal of the architecture of the colonies. It has been said that colonial architecture fits into no single logical category, and that in consequence no assessment is realistically possible. This is an arbitrary and somewhat narrow-minded summing-up of an architectural conundrum that needs only the application of a little imagination. If we are, however, to take the line that there is no 'Colonial' style, as there is an 'Anglo-Palladian' and a 'Picturesque' style, then the imperial constructions are English and should be included in the corpus of English architecture. If they defy this categorization, then perhaps they should be subdivided by country or by style – Victorian, Georgian, or Regency. There is plenty of choice. Certainly historians in many of the major countries of the British Empire have written a huge number of books on a subject which has, to date, been beyond the scope of Britain's own authors. This should be qualified by acknowledging that their works have always been confined to their own countries without any attempt at comparison. There can be few fields of architecture which are more difficult to compare for reasons of physical location and lack of documentation, but this again defines the problem and not the answer. It is evident that there are no simple answers, and that the buildings of the British Empire form a vast body of architecture that has been largely ignored by the very people whose country was its catalyst and whose heritage was its principal inspiration.

Bibliography

Acworth, A.C., *Treasure in the Caribbean*, London 1949

Adamson, A., *The Gaiety of Gables*, Toronto 1973

Allen, C., *Plain Tales from the Raj*, London 1975

—*Tales from the Dark Continent*, London 1981

—*Tales from the China Seas*, London 1983

Amery, C., *Lutyens*, exh. cat., London 1982

Andrews, W., *Architecture in New England*, Brattleboro, Vermont 1973

Angus, M., *The Old Stones of Kingston: Its Buildings before 1867*, Toronto 1966

anon., *Life in Bombay*, London 1887

Architects' Emergency Committee, *Great Georgian Houses of America*, New York 1970

Arthur, E.R., *Small Houses of the Late 18th and Early 19th Centuries in Ontario*, Toronto 1932

—*The Early Buildings of Ontario*, Toronto 1938

—*Toronto: No Mean City*, Toronto 1964

Atkinson, G.F., *Curry and Rice*, London 1859

Australian Council of National Trusts, *Historic Public Buildings of Australia*, North Ryde, New South Wales 1971

Baker, H., *Cecil Rhodes by His Architect*, London 1934

Baker, N.B., *Early Houses of New England*, Rutland, Vermont 1980

Ballhatchet, K. and Harrison, J., eds., *The City in South Asia, Pre-Modern and Modern*, Collected Papers on South Asia, IV. 3, London 1980

Barrett, K., 'Railway trains of the Raj', *Namaskar* (Air India Journal), Hong Kong Apr./May 1982

Basia, J. and Robatch, P., *Prints of South-East Asia in the India Office Library*, London 1982

Beloff, Max, *The Rise and Fall of the Second British Empire: India, Africa and Australia*, London 1982

Bence-Jones, M., *Palaces of the Raj*, London 1973

Beresford-Hope, A.J.B., *The English Cathedral in the Nineteenth Century*, London 1961

Binney, M. and Pearce, D., eds., *Railway Architecture*, London 1979

Blake, V.B. and Greenhill, R., *Rural Ontario*, Toronto 1969

Brousseau, M., 'Gothic Revival in Canadian architecture', *Canadian Historic Sites: Occasional Papers in Archaeology and History*, no. 25, Ottawa 1980

Burnett, A. and Yule, H., *Hobson-Jobson*, 2nd edn. London 1903

Butcher, J.G., *The British in Malaya, 1880–1941*, 1979

Buttlar, A.V., *Der englische Landsitz, 1715–1760*, Mittenwald 1982

Buyers, M. and others, *Rural Roots: Pre-Confederation Buildings of the York Region of Ontario*, Toronto 1976

Cameron, C. and Trudel, J., *The Drawings of James Cockburn: A Visit through Quebec's Past*, Toronto 1976

Cameron, R., *Shadows from India*, London 1958

Casey, M. and others, *Early Melbourne Architecture, 1840–1888*, Melbourne 1953

Chin, L., *Cultural Heritage of Sarawak*, Kuching 1981

Chinatown, An Album of a Singapore Community, Singapore 1983

Clarke, Basil F.L., *Cathedrals outside the British Isles*, London 1958

Collins, M., *Raffles*, London 1966

Cox, P. and Stacey, W., *The Australian Homestead*, Melbourne 1972

Cummings, A.L., *The Framed Houses of Massachusetts Bay (1625–1735)*, Cambridge, Massachusetts 1979

Darby, M., *The Islamic Perspective*, London 1983

Darwent, Rev. C.E., *Shanghai, A Handbook for Travellers*, Shanghai 1905

Desmond, R., *Photography in South Asia during the Nineteenth Century*, London 1974

—*Victorian India in Focus*, London 1982

'disappearing town houses of Hong Kong, The', *The Peninsula Group Magazine*, Hong Kong 25 April 1982

Doig, Desmond, *Calcutta*, Calcutta 1968

Dupain, M., *Georgian Architecture of Australia*, Sydney 1963

Eberlein, H.D. and Hubbard, C.V.D., *American Georgian Architecture*, London 1952

Edwardes, M., *British India*, London 1967

—*Bound to Exile*, London 1969

—*A Remote Élite*, London 1972

Ellis, M.H., *Francis Greenway*, Sydney 1953

Encyclopaedia Britannica, 1970, vol. x.

'End of an era in Hong Kong', *The Peninsula Group Magazine*, Hong Kong 25 April 1982

Eyre & Hobhouse Ltd., *Bengal: Palladian and the Picturesque – Colonial Architecture in the Indian Landscape, 1780–1980*, exh. cat., London 1982

Fergusson, J., *History of the Modern Styles of Architecture*, vol. IV, London 1873

Finckenstaedt, Th., *Der Garten des Königs, in Problems der Kunstwissenschaft*, Berlin 1966

Fogg's Weekly Journal, no. 128, 26 June 1731

Forbes, J., *Oriental Memoirs*, vol. 4, London 1813

Fox, J. *White Mischief*, London 1982

Freeland, J.M., *Architecture of Australia*, Melbourne 1968

Freeman, A.F., *Railways: Past, Present and Future*, London 1983

Gauthier, R., *Les Manoirs du Québec*, Quebec 1976

Gowman, A., *Building Canada: An Architectural History of Canadian Life*, Toronto 1966

Greenberger, A.J., *The British Image of India*, London 1969

Greenhill, R., *The Face of Toronto*, Oxford 1960

—and Macpherson, K. and Richardson, D., *Ontario Towns*, Ottawa 1974

Greenough, J.J., 'The Halifax Citadel, 1825–60, a narrative and structural history', *Canadian Historic Sites: Occasional Papers in Archaeology and History*, no. 17, Ottawa 1977

Grieg, D.E., *Herbert Baker in South Africa*, Cape Town 1970

Hall-Jones, J., *An Early Surveyor in Singapore: John Turnbull-Thomson, Singapore 1841–53*, Singapore 1979

Hamshere, C., 'Hunting the Georgian', *Apollo*, London 1971

— *The British in the Caribbean*, London 1972

Hancock, T.H.H., ed., *Quarterly Journal of the Institute of Architects of Malaya*, 1951–6

—'Coleman in Singapore', *Architectural Review*, London 1955

—'Singaporiana', *Architectural Association Journal*, London 1955

—'City Boulevard – Queen Elizabeth Walk', *Straits Times Annual*, Singapore 1956

—'The House in Coleman Street', *Straits Times Press*, Singapore 1956

—*Coleman's Singapore in Retrospect*, 1984

—and Gibson-Hill, C.A., *Architecture in Singapore*, 1954

Hawksmoor, N., letter to Earl of Carlisle, quoted in Buttlar, q.v.

Head, R., 'From Obsession to Obscurity: Colonel R.Smith, Architect and Engineer', *Country Life*, London May 1981

Heritage Trust of Nova Scotia, ed., *Founded Upon a Rock: Historic Buildings of Halifax and Vicinity Standing in 1967*, Halifax 1967

—*Seasoned Timbers: A Sampling of Historic Buildings Unique to Western Nova Scotia*, 2nd edn. Halifax 1972

Hill, M., *Permanent Way* (official history of the Kenya-Uganda Railway), Nairobi 1976

History Around Us, Hong Kong 1982

History of Discovery and Exploration: Eastern Islands and Southern Seas, London 1973

Hong Kong Album, The, Hong Kong 1982

Hubbard, R.H., 'Canadian Gothic', *Architectural Review*, vol. 116, no. 8, London Aug. 1954

— *The Development of Canadian Art*, Ottawa 1963

—'The European Backgrounds of Early Canadian Art', *Art Quarterly*, XXVII, 1964

Hume, I.N., *Martin's Hundred*, London 1983

Humphreys, B.A., 'The architectural heritage of the Rideau Corridor', *Canadian Historic Sites: Occasional Papers in Archaeology and History*, no. 10, Ottawa 1974

Huxley, E., *White Man's Country*, London 1935

—*Four Guineas*, London 1954

—*The Flame Trees of Thika*, London 1959

—*White Man's Country: Lord Delamere and the Making of Kenya*, London 1968

—*Nellie, Letters from Africa*, London 1980

Indian Freemason, The, Calcutta 1896

Irving, R.G., *Indian Summer – Lutyens, Baker and Imperial Delhi*, London/New Haven 1981

Isaac, R., *The Transformation of Virginia 1740–1790*, Chapel Hill, North Carolina 1983

Jensen, E. and R., *Colonial Architecture in South Australia*, Adelaide 1980

Jizuka, K., *Calcutta: The Formation of the British Colonial City*, unpublished Ph.D. thesis, Tokyo University 1980

Johnson, D.L., *Australian Architecture (1905–51): Sources of Modernism*, Sydney 1980

Judd, D., *The Victorian Empire*, London 1983

Kaye, M.M., ed., *The Golden Calm, an English Lady's Life in Moghul Delhi*, New York 1980

— *The Far Pavilions Picture Book*, London 1979

Kearney, B., *Architecture in Natal from 1824–93*, Cape Town 1973

Kennedy, L., *A Book of Air Journeys*, London 1982

—*A Book of Railway Journeys*, London 1982

Keswick, M., *The Thistle and the Jade: A Celebration of Jardine, Matheson & Co.*, London 1982

Kettel, R.H., *Early American Rooms: 1650–1858*, New York 1968

Kimball, F., *Domestic Architecture of the American Colonies and of the Early Republic*, New York 1966

Kincaid, D., *British Social Life in India (1608–1937)*, London 1939

King, A.D., 'The bungalow', *Architectural Association Quarterly*, vol. 5, no. 3, London 1973

—*Colonial Urban Development: Culture, Social Power and Environment*, 1976

—'The Bengali peasant hut', *Art and Archaeology Research Papers*, Dec. 1977

Kingsley, M., *Travels in West Africa*, London 1982
Kipling, R., *The Light that Failed*, London 1895

Lake, E., *Plans and Views Illustrating the Journals of the Sieges of the Madras Army*, London 1825.
Leary, F. and J., *Colonial Heritage: Historic Buildings of New South Wales*, Sydney 1972
Lewcock, R., *Early Nineteenth Century Architecture in South Africa*, Cape Town 1963
Lochee, L., *An Essay on Castramentation*, London 1778
Lotus International, no. 26, ed. D. Jones, Milan 1980
—no. 34, Milan 1982
Loudon, J., *Treatise on Country Residences*, London 1806
Lucas, C., *Colonial Architecture*, Melbourne 1978

Macdonald, S., *Sally in Rhodesia*, Bulawayo 1970
Macmillan, A., *East Africa and Rhodesia, Their Civilization, Resources etc.*, 1931
Macmillan Encyclopaedia of Architects, 4 vols., New York 1982
MacRae, M., *The Ancestral Roof: Domestic Architecture of Upper Canada*, Toronto 1975
'Malayan Civil Service: colonial bureaucracy/bureaucratic élite', *Comparative Studies of Society and History*, 12.2, Cambridge 1970
Marsan, C., *Montréal en évolution*, Montreal 1974
Metcalfe, T., 'Architecture and Empire', *History Today*, London July 1980
—'A tradition created: Indo-Saracenic architecture under the Raj', *History Today*, London Sept. 1982
Miller, C., *The Lunatic Express*, London 1982
Moorehead, A., *The Blue Nile*, London 1962
—*The White Nile*, London 1980
Moorhouse, G., *Calcutta: The City Revealed*, London 1983
—*India Britannica*, London 1983
Morgan, E.J.R. and Gilbert, S.H., *Early Adelaide Architecture (1830–86)*, London 1970
Morris, J., *Pax Britannica*, London 1968
—*Heaven's Command*, London 1973
—*Farewell the Trumpets*, London 1978
—*The Spectacle of Empire*, London 1982
—*Stones of Empire*, London 1984
Morrison, H., *Early American Architecture from the First Colonial Settlements to the National Period*, London & New York 1953
Murray, H., *British India*, n.p., vol 2, London & Edinburgh 1850
Murray, J., *A Handbook for India, Burma and Ceylon*, 4th edn., London 1901
Murray's Handbook, London 1847

Nankivell, J., 'Heritage of the Raj: drawings of Madras', *Architectural Review*, London 1974
New Brunswick Provincial Archives, *Fredericton: The Early Years*, photographic exh. cat., Fredericton, New Brunswick 1974
Newfoundland Historic Trust, *A Gift of Heritage*, St John's 1975
Nichols, H., *Exploration and the First British Empire: Settlement and Colonisation in the New World*, London 1982
Nicholson, C.A., 'Notes on Australian architecture', *Architectural Review*, London
Nicholson, Peter, *The New and Improved Practical Builder*, London 1823
Nilsson, S., *European Architecture in India (1750–1850)*, London 1968
Noppen, L., *Les Églises du Québec (1600–1850)*, Montreal 1974
—'Le Rôle de l'Abbé Jérôme Demers dans l'élaboration d'une architecture néo-classique au Québec', *Journal of Canadian Art History*, vol. 2, no. 1, Montreal summer 1975
—and Paulette, C. and Tremblay, M., *Québec: Trois siècles d'architecture*, Quebec 1979
Norberg-Schulz, C., *Genius Loci: Towards a Phenomenology of Architecture*, London 1980

Ondaatje, K. and Mackenzie, L., *Old Ontario Houses*, Toronto 1977
'Onwards and eastwards: Western influenced architecture of the 19th and 20th Century', *Art and Archaeology Research Papers*, no. 11, June 1977
Orwell, G., *Burmese Days*, Harmondsworth 1957 (1st edn. London 1934)

Padfield P., *Beneath the House Flag of the PO*, London 1982
Palladio, A., *The Four Books of Architecture*, ed. Isaac Ware, London 1738
Parr and Desmond, *Simla, A British Hill Station*, London 1977
Pasco, C.F., *Two Hundred Years of the Society for the Propagation of the Gospel*, London 1901
Pearson, R., *Eastern Interlude: A Social History of the European Community in Calcutta*, 1954
Pedler, F., *The Lion and the Unicorn in Africa*, London 1974
Perham, M., *African Apprenticeship*, London 1974
—*East African Journey*, London 1975
Petricioni, H., 'Das neue Arkadien', in *Europäische Bukolik und Georgik*, ed. K. Garber, Darmstadt 1976
Pevsner, Nikolaus, 'The genesis of the Picturesque', *Architectural Review*, London Nov. 1944
Picton-Seymour, D., *Victorian Buildings in South Africa, Including Edwardian and Transvaal Republican Styles*, Cape Town 1977
Pieper, J., *The Mofussil Environment: Elements of Colonial Architecture and Settlement in Up-Country India*
—*Die anglo-indische Station*, Bonn 1975
Pierson, W.H., Jr, *American Buildings and their Architects, vol. 1: The Colonial and Neo-Classical Styles*, New York 1970
Playne, S., *East Africa and Its Resources*, London 1908
Pott, J., *Old Bungalows in Bangalore*, London 1977
Priceless Heritage: Historic Buildings of Tasmania, Hobart 1971
Pudney, J., *The Thomas Cook Story*, London 1953

Rempel, J.I., *Building with Wood and Other Aspects of Nineteenth-Century*

Building in Central Canada, rev. Edn., Toronto 1980

Richardson, D., 'Hyperborean Gothic: or wilderness ecclesiology and the wood churches of Edward Medley', *Architectura*, vol. 2, no. 1, Munich Jan. 1972

—'The Spirit of Place', *Canadian Antiques Collection*, vol. 10, no. 5, Sept.-Oct. 1975.

Ritchie, T. and Arthur, E., *Iron: Cast and Wrought Iron in Canada from the Seventeenth Century to the Present*, Toronto 1982

Robertson, E.G., *Early Buildings of Southern Tamania*, 2 vols., London 1970

—and Robertson, J., *Cast Iron Decoration: A World Survey*, London 1977

Robson, L.L., *The Convict Settlers of Australia*, London & Melbourne 1965

Rolleston, S.E., *Heritage Houses: The American Tradition in Connecticut (1660–1900)*, New York 1979

Ronnie, J., *The Buildings of Central Cape Town*, Cape Town 1978

Royal Asiatic Society (Malaysian Branch), *Coleman's Singapore in Retrospect*, Petaling Jaya, Malaysia 1984

Satow, H. and Ray, D., *Railways of the Raj*, London 1980

Sharp, I., *There Is Only One Raffles*, London 1982

Shore, J.F., *Indian Affairs*, London 1837

Singapore: A Guide Book, Singapore 1983

Smith, R., *Australia's Historical Heritage: The Birth of a Nation*, South Yarra, New South Wales 1981

Sorrenson, M.P.R., *European Settlement in Kenya, Origins of*, Nairobi 1968

Southey, R., quoted in Santapau, H., *Common Trees of India*, Delhi 1966

Stacpoole, J. and Beaver, P., *New Zealand Art and Architecture, 1820–1970*, Wellington 1972

Staley, E., *Monkeytops: Old Buildings in Bangalore Cantonment*, London 1981

Stamp, G., *1900*, exh. cat., London 1975

—'Indian Summer', *Architectural Review*, London June 1976

—'British Architecture in India: 1857–1947', *Royal Society of Arts Journal*, CXXIX, London May 1981

Stanford, J.K., *Ladies in the Sun: Memsahib's India (1760–1860)*, London 1962

Stewart, J.D., 'Architecture for a boomtown: the primitive and neo-Baroque in George Brown's Kingston buildings', in G. Tulchinsky, *To Preserve and Defend: Essays on Kingston in the Nineteenth Century*, Montreal 1976

—and Wilson, I.E., *Heritage Kingston*, Kingston 1973

Stokes, P., *Old Niagara on the Lake*, Toronto 1971

Summerson, J., *British Architecture 1530–1830*, London 1953

Tarapor, M., 'Growse in Bulandshahr', *Architectural Review*, London Sept. 1982

—*John Lockwood Kipling and the Arts and Crafts Movement in India*, lecture at Architectural Association School, London 23 March 1982

Taylor, A., *Laurence Oliphant, 1829–88*, Oxford 1982

Thompson, H.P., *Into All Lands, The History of the Society for the Propagation of the Gospel*, London 1901

Tindall, G., *City of Gold: The Biography of Bombay*, London 1982

van Ryssen, E., 'John Parker's Cape Town', *Argus Magazine*, Cape Town 16 Oct. 1982

'Villes Coloniales', *URBI*, ed. D.Jones, Paris Dec. 1982

Traguair, R., *The Old Architecture of Quebec*, Toronto 1947

Vibart, H.M., *Military History of the Madras Engineers*, London 1881

Waterman, T.T., *The Dwellings of Colonial America*, 1979

Weeks, S., *Decaying Splendours*, London 1979

Westwater, N., 'European influences in the architecture of the Sudan in the time of Kitchener and his successors', *Art and Archaeology Research Papers*, London 1984

Whiffen, M. and Koeper, F., *American Architecture 1607–1976*, Cambridge (Mass.) 1981

Wills, F., *Ancient English Ecclesiastical Architecture and its Principles, Applied to the Wants of the Church at the Present Day*, 1850

Wilson, A., *R.Kipling*, London 1977

Winchester, S., 'The Loneliest outpost: St Helena', *Sunday Times*. London July 1983

Woodcock, G., *The British in the Far East*, 1969

Worwick, C., *The Last Empire: Photography in British India, 1855–1911*, London 1976

Index